Work With Purpose:
Fifty Years of Supported Employment and Training in the Annapolis Valley

Jim Prime

Work With Purpose: Fifty Years of Supported Employment and Training in the Annapolis Valley
Copyright © 2020 The Flower Cart Group
Written by Jim Prime   ISBN: 9798592365089

Layout and cover design by:
CLAIRMONT PUBLISHING SERVICES
5720 Prospect Rd New Minas, NS B4N 3K6

CONTENTS

Disclaimer:
This book features historically accurate quotations and terminology that is now considered antiquated or offensive. The inclusion of these phrases or words is in no way an indication that The Flower Cart Group condones their use, but it recognizes that there is an important opportunity to reflect on the evolution of language and perception, particularly in the field of disability supports. It has been a fifty-year effort to enhance supports for persons with disabilities in Kings County and it is important not to gloss over or omit the less palatable parts of that history.

This book is dedicated to all the men and women of The Flower Cart Group, those amazing staff, participants, board members, and other volunteers whose selfless devotion to the service of others left an indelible mark on the history of the organization and is responsible for an enduring legacy of compassion, hope, and resilience.

INTRODUCTION

The Flower Cart was built on the core belief that every person has value and the right to meaningful employment. These fundamental tenets were set out in a 1974 mission statement and have served as the driving force for the organization for fifty years:

In response to a need for a training facility for the post-school developmentally handicapped in East King's County, the Flower Cart Activity Training Centre was opened in the fall of 1970 under the sponsorship of The Canadian Association for the Mentally Retarded, King's County Branch. In 1973, it became an incorporated body under The Societies Act of Nova Scotia and, while participating in C.A.M.R. activities, is autonomous in that its administrative and program policies are the prerogative of its Board of Directors.

Sheltered workshops play an important role in the national, provincial and municipal planning for the developmentally handicapped young adults and bridge the gap from school to requirements of society, industry, and the family enabling them to participate in family and community living, and hopefully for some, earn a living in the social environment in which they live.

The trainees, like all other individuals, differ from one another intellectually, socially, emotionally, and physically. Society expects the developmentally handicapped of post-school age, as it does others, to assume as many adult responsibilities as they possibly can. However, there is a great variation among the developmentally handicapped, especially in their personal, social, and vocational ability and adjustment.

There are some who are able to assume adult responsibilities with little post-school training. Others have some skills for adult living but lack the necessary vocational skills and good work habits needed for employment, either sheltered or competitive. Then, there are some post-school developmentally handicapped who are unable to make the transition into adult living without the help of specialized training and will require on a long-term basis an activity program and/or a sheltered work environment.

Institutions and services for the handicapped are changing, and so are prejudices and public attitudes. There is an international movement, both on the part of the mentally handicapped themselves and for them towards independence under the "principles of normalization" - which simply means making available to them the patterns and conditions of everyday life which are as close as possible to the normal rhythm of the day, a normal routine of the week, including work and leisure time activities, and opportunity to undergo the developmental experiences of the life cycle.

Because of a somewhat limited population with its related limitations of finance, personnel, and transportation, The Flower Cart program strives to operate a coordinated comprehensive program of activity centre, sheltered workshop, and vocational training with the help and cooperation of volunteers, consultants, and community organizations and agencies.

The program starts at the level of performance related to the simplest of adult living skills and progresses to the point where these young people are able to assume increasing adult responsibilities more in line with their chronological adulthood through an evolving program to modify behaviour, acquire new skills to enable them to reach and maintain a higher level of functioning, learn to separate from families, master self-care skills and self-travel, to participate in peer-group activities and to relate to non-parent, non-teacher adults and to make wise use of leisure time aimed at using the resources of regular society.

Recreation and social activities have a high priority in the program so that an acceptable pattern of daily social living can be developed while still providing for satisfying necessary work experiences and vocational training.

From its initiation, the Board has felt this project should be community oriented and today, after four years of operation, feels even stronger in this regard. Without the support of interested community people and organizations working closely with the trainees, staff and administration, the long-term goals of integration and normalization cannot be achieved. The project has received strong and encouraging acceptance from the community and a solid foundation has been laid to support future growth in enriching and broadening programs to provide a full circle of life-time services for and possibly from the developmentally handicapped.

It is the hope of the Board that, as funds permit, a long-term remunerative sheltered work project (i.e. industry operated by the trainees, farm, etc.) can be established for those who are not capable of full-time employment on the open competitive labour market, but who are capable of productive activities in a sheltered environment which will enable these young people to demonstrate their ability to be useful members of society.

It is also their hope that in the near future, community residences can be established to enable these young people to further demonstrate their ability to be less dependent on others and to enjoy a more normal and meaningful way of life.

After several years of operation, during which time we have all gained experience, understanding, and insight into the many and varied problems of such a comprehensive program, it is the hope of the Board of Directors that the information contained herein may be a valuable guide to future members, staff and volunteers and serve as a framework of reference for policy and personnel practices and for structuring future programs.

- The Board of Directors, 1974

This simple but powerful creed has remained a lodestar throughout the Flower Cart's history, shaping policy for successive administrations and serving as a motivator for staff and participants alike. The terminology has changed but the principles remain, and the vision articulated in this mission statement has proven solid enough to endure and timeless enough to encompass societal changes.

With thousands of cars passing by its doors every day, The Flower Cart, located on Commercial Street in New Minas is blessed with high visibility and yet few people know of its vision, or the succession of visionaries who have made it an integral part of the surrounding Annapolis Valley community. The building that has housed the thriving enterprise throughout its first five decades is unassuming, bordering on nondescript, and there are few exterior clues about what goes on behind these walls. Even the name on the sign, The Flower Cart Group, is ambiguous at best and a scattered array of secondary signage suggests only that the activities within are many and varied.

The result is that, despite the integral role it plays in all sectors of our community, the multi-faceted organization is hidden in plain sight. The Flower Cart is now fifty years old, an appropriate time for looking back to its beginnings, exploring its history and accomplishments, and looking forward to the next fifty years.

Every worthwhile venture starts with a clear and well-defined vision, and a core group of dedicated individuals with the will and sheer audacity to make it work. In the case of The Flower Cart, the core beliefs are those laid out in the above document, beginning with the assertion that everyone has the right to meaningful work. The believers were Jean DeWolfe, her husband Owen, and a pioneering cadre of Wolfville women.

Jean and Owen's daughter Linda was born with Down syndrome and, following a year in public school, attended the NS Training School in Truro until the age of 18, at which point she was no longer eligible. She returned home to the Valley and an uncertain future because Kings County – and Nova Scotia in general – had little or nothing to offer adults like Linda.

Nothing focuses the mind quite like desperation, especially when your own child is involved, and Jean set out to remedy an untenable situation. She wanted Linda to enjoy, as much as possible, a range of life experiences that other young women took for granted, to assume adult responsibilities, and to reach her potential as a productive member of society. These specific goals for her daughter evolved and expanded to include all Kings County adults with intellectual disabilities.

The Flower Cart opened in September of 1970 to Linda and four other female clients. Over the next few months, the former New Minas Elementary School was transformed into an activity centre dedicated to work-related training for adults with intellectual disabilities.

During its five decades, it has grown in both scope and impact, enriching the lives of countless Valley people - and not only those who have passed through the doors as participants. The Flower Cart's role is multi-faceted. It has partnered with the business community to the mutual benefit of both. It's a training centre, a marketplace, a developer of qualified workers for specialized tasks, a problem solver for entrepreneurs. It's a training centre that allows participants to enter the work force and a provider of goods and services to the region.

MISCONCEPTIONS

Despite its longevity and the deep roots it has put down in the community, many misconceptions about The Flower Cart remain. It's time to dispel those misconceptions and provide an accurate accounting of what it is and what it is not. For starters, it's not a florist or a greenhouse; i.e., flowers are not sold there.

It's not a warehouse for people, nor is it a place of frivolous "busy work." It's not an institution and the atmosphere isn't gloomy. In fact, quite the opposite. It's a hive of activity: vibrant and full of energy, focus, creativity, and productivity. There is nothing random or chaotic about the activity, it is purpose-driven. The Flower Cart has exacting standards and strict bylaws that are enforced by staff and fellow trainees.

The participants are engaged and motivated, regardless of their ability level. They are not children and they are not treated as children. The staff are not baby sitters. They are experienced professionals, skilled in organization and schooled in the latest pedagogy. They are hired for their competence, their caring, and their commitment to putting the client first. The participants are mentored, encouraged, and treated with respect. Their opinions are actively sought out and listened to. Many can work independently, others require more attention and assistance. The programmes are designed to reflect this range of intellectual ability. They take individual and collective pride in their work and in The Flower Cart.

Participants don't live at The Flower Cart. They come in and they participate in training and they get paid for work. Many participants have families and jobs outside of The Flower Cart environment. They pay taxes, do volunteer work, and generally contribute to the community.

WHAT'S IN A NAME?

The Flower Cart has always welcomed visitors and loves to spotlight its participants and programs. In an effort to make the organization more transparent, Executive Director Jeff Kelly has made it his mission to educate and inform the public. It was felt that a name change might further the cause.

"Before I became executive director of The Flower Cart, I was familiar with the sector of our community it served. Even then, I knew that there were lots of misconceptions and stereotypes that went with the brand, so when I met with the board of directors to get our Building Opportunities Capital Campaign underway, I thought that the campaign offered an opportunity to rebrand the organization with a name that better reflected what we do.

"I hoped that a new name would start to break down the stereotypes that exist – that it's not, in fact, an organization where disabled kids go and work on arts and crafts. We've never had children, only adults. In fact, we have one gentleman who is two years younger than my dad - but some people still assume he's with disabled kids. I wanted to rename in order to clarify our role. I wanted to get rid of the Flower Cart name and rebrand us. When I pitched my proposal to the board, the response was lukewarm, and the staff was evenly split on the concept. I'd never run a capital campaign but a large part of the fundraising consists of large gift acquisitions, so I consulted with a group that assists philanthropic organizations with such campaigns. They advised against the name change.

"They pointed out that everybody knows the Flower Cart name and even though they may be unclear about exactly what we do, a very positive name recognition comes with it. Going into a major fundraising campaign, the timing might be bad for introducing a name no one knows. I compromised and in retrospect I'm glad now that it didn't happen."

FINDING A NEW HOME

Like many dynamic enterprises, The Flower Cart has outgrown its premises. There are too many participants, too many programmes, too many activities for the old New Minas Elementary to house. The Building Opportunities Capital Campaign is currently underway to build a beautiful new facility just up the road on the opposite side of Commercial Street. This new complex will make The Flower Cart even more visible and much more accessible to the general public. It's designed not only to showcase the array of activities that participants are involved in but to draw the general public and area entrepreneurs to their doors for a variety of consumer experiences and game-changing new business opportunities.

Since its conversion into a training centre, the existing building has undergone numerous physical changes and additions and has served its purpose well. It has produced bakers and carpenters and taught a variety of other skills, both social and practical. Its alumni can be found in workplaces throughout the Valley. Without knowing it, you likely see and interact with them every day. They work in factories and coffee shops and medical facilities and retail outlets. They are raising families, paying taxes, and contributing to society. They are part of the fabric of our community.

The new facility will provide the resources and space needed to accommodate increased enrollment and innovative new programming options. It will offer the community a variety of goods and services and deconstruct misconceptions about who they are and what they do.

The Building Opportunities Project includes the construction of a 23,000-square foot building next door to the Louis Millett Community Complex in New Minas. After several years of planning, the capital campaign was launched in the spring of 2018 and stakeholders have been consulted on an ongoing basis. Most notably, participants have offered input on components and programs that are factors in the design. The process has been lengthy and at times challenging, but it has already brought rewards.

"We exist for the participants that we support and not vice versa," Jeff Kelly told the Kentville Advertiser. "They've been with us every step of the way as an included partner and stakeholder group. They're been given the opportunity and a measure of respect as we ask, 'What do you think about this? Will this work for you?'"

Completion date is set for the spring of 2021 with a price tag of $5.6 million. Among the many unique features is a new social enterprise, a 1600 sq. ft community hub with open space, offices and board rooms. It will serve as a coworking space for business people and entrepreneurs who usually work from home. Kelly sees it as a win-win concept where ideally, "We would incubate entrepreneurs and then do business with them."

SHAWN BIGGS, A PROFILE

Shawn Biggs sits at the kitchen table of his immaculate New Minas apartment, his wife Cindy at his side. Shawn is a man of great dignity and presence. He's eager to tell his story but often defers to Cindy regarding specific dates and other details. Shawn has brain cancer. A surgical scar on his head is the only physical evidence of his ordeal.

Over coffee, his incredible story unfolds. It's a story about overcoming adversity and the key role The Flower Cart has played in his life. Shawn is not a complainer, nor is he wrapped in self-pity. He's thankful that he has a loving partner and proud of what he's been able to accomplish in his life.

Ironically, Shawn's father died of brain cancer after being exposed to Agent Orange while stationed at CFB Gagetown in New Brunswick. "My father had taught me to have respect for others and have respect for yourself," he says. "He passed that down to me. He was very regimental, a good man, a great man." In 1994, Shawn, then 22 years of age, was working at an

East Side Mario's in Ottawa when he suffered a seizure. Quick action by his brother-in-law saved his life, but his doctors gave him only a fifty percent chance of survival. He would go on to undergo thirty-six rounds of radiotherapy.

He returned to Nova Scotia and found employment at Paddy's Pub in Kentville but after experiencing repeated seizures, underwent chemotherapy. What followed were frequent visits to Halifax to consult with a battery of specialists. Shawn remarkably maintained a positive outlook. "He was a real leader and had an amazing positivity," says Cindy. "He's been through so much hell and never once complained. Virtually everyone who mentions the name Shawn Biggs, includes the descriptors natural leader and role model."

The regimen of invasive treatments and procedures halted the progress of the cancer, but they also took a toll on his memory and some motor skills. Despite his best efforts to find a job, he was deemed unable to work in most professions. For a man with his strong work ethic, the situation was devastating. It was at this low point that The Flower Cart offered a ray of hope.

In 2003, Lisa Hammett-Vaughn was supervising The Flower Cart's outreach program, Partners in Employment (PIE), when Shawn dropped by to check it out. "Shawn was amazing," Lisa recalls. "He was a bit different from a lot of people we worked with because he wasn't born handicapped. He had brain cancer – which means brain injury basically – and had lost some abilities. He'd been a chef working with knives but his dexterity was deteriorating and sometimes he would just drop things. He was having mild seizures and dropping knives so they told him he couldn't work in the kitchen anymore." Shawn knew that his job options were shrinking. "There were too many things to remember working in restaurant kitchens," he says.

Hammett-Vaughn saw him as an ideal candidate for the PIE program and specifically the partnership that had been established with the Michelin Tire plant in Waterville. "The job seemed ideally suited to him," she says. "So, he went to Michelin on contract and was stripping tires – peeling rubber apart to reclaim it. And he could work harder, faster, and with more enthusiasm than anyone, so he was a natural leader and people looked up to him. He set the tone and the pace and he would tell people when he didn't think they were being safe."

"At Michelin it was all repetition and following the rules," Shawn says. "I concentrated totally on the job and safety. Didn't take my stress to work. My motto was: 'When at home, keep your stresses at home. When at work, give it 110%.' I think that had an influence on my fellow workers. I loved being a role model."

There were times when his dedication was nothing less than heroic, as he underwent an eight-week course of chemotherapy to contain the cancer. During that time his weight dropped from 210 pounds to 160. "My philosophy was that if you can walk and talk, I'm still working," Shawn says.

"He never gave up," Cindy says. "He'd get nauseous from the chemo and go to the washroom and throw up then come back and keep working at peeling tires. And then after work, he'd go home and have more chemo."

For Shawn it was the work that kept him going. He loved the challenge and took pride in a job well done. "We were tearing apart winter, spring, and fall tires, separating them, and the regular workers couldn't keep up with us," he says. "I was the leader and it made me feel so good. They even gave me a blue t-shirt to show that I was leader of these guys. It was one step up for me – like a promotion was for my father."

One day, Cindy was surprised to see Shawn arrive home early with his boss who explained that Shawn had suffered a seizure at work. Due to safety concerns, there was no choice but to terminate his employment. The event signalled the end of his working days. "I was so sad," he says. "I loved Michelin."

Now 48, Shawn looks back on his struggles philosophically, thankful to have the love and support of his wife and the respect that he earned through the Partners in Employment program at Michelin. And thankful to be alive. "The doctor told him more than once, 'Shawn, you shouldn't be here,'" says Cindy.

Following his retirement, Lisa Hammett-Vaughn took the stage at the Union Street Café in Berwick to honour Shawn. She introduced him and praised him as a role model, and leader whose positivity was contagious. "Her words were so touching," Cindy says. "I cried through the whole thing."

THE BIGGS AWARD

Shawn Biggs is just one of countless adults with intellectual disabilities whose lives have been enriched through the support of The Flower Cart. Because his story embodies The Flower Cart's creed that every life has value and everyone has the right to challenging employment, it was decided that an annual award be created bearing his name.

Lisa Hammett-Vaughan explains the origins of the Biggs Award: "There were so many great stories to be told by and about our clients. I suggested to (then executive director) Roger Tatlock that we should try to find a way to tell them. That's how it started in 2004. The names of recommended candidates came from employers who wanted one of their workers to be recognized. Of course, when you work with a person who has a disability a lot of information is private and we're always trying to preserve their dignity. Some don't want to be singled out but every year we have a winner. I can still drive up and down the Valley and remember past winners who worked at various places."

Appropriately, the initial winner of the Biggs Award, presented at an emotional ceremony on June 15, 2004, was the inspirational Shawn Biggs, who fit the criteria perfectly:

> *The award identifies a person who demonstrates the work skills taught and supported by Flower Cart Community Employment Services. It highlights workers who have cognitive disabilities and who have become excellent role models for others. The Biggs Award makes clear to the community the kind of worker that Flower Cart values. In addition to offering employers a way of recognizing outstanding employees, it also allows The Flower Cart an opportunity to recognize its employer partners.*

A decade and half later, Hammett-Vaughn still remembers Shawn coming to work at Michelin between bouts of chemo despite the extreme side effects of the drug. "I kept saying to him, 'Are you sure you should be here?', and he'd say, 'Oh, yeah, I can do it.' He lost a ton of weight but he really wanted to work. It was really sad when they finally told him that his condition had crossed the line and he couldn't come anymore. For years after that he still hoped he was going to improve to the point where he would be able to return."

The Biggs Award is what The Flower Cart is all about: it recognizes the value and dignity of purposeful work and the inherent value of every individual, regardless of their ability. As Lisa Hammett-Vaughn put it so well when describing Shawn Biggs, "He was a different kind of being, that's for sure."

CHAPTER ONE: THE WAY IT WAS

To fully understand and appreciate what The Flower Cart has meant to adults with intellectual disabilities, it's necessary to delve into a dark period in Nova Scotia's history.

Those who have visited The Flower Cart have seen the open and respectful interaction between participants and staff. They have listened to the buzz of activity, and noted the good humour, teamwork, and positivity that fills the place. There is a sense of purpose and pride of workmanship that is impossible to miss. In such a setting, it's easy to forget that prior to 1970 there were no services in Kings County (or anywhere else in Nova Scotia) for adults considered to have intellectual disabilities. No programs to inspire and challenge, no sense of satisfaction for a job well done. No hope that they could become productive members of society.

Not so long ago, poor houses were familiar sights strategically positioned across the Nova Scotia landscape. They could be found in virtually every county in the province, with some jurisdictions boasting more than one. Many of these structures were Dickensian in appearance and they all reflected a societal mindset not unlike the one that Charles Dickens wrote about so compellingly.

From their very inception, the term poor house was something of a misnomer. These government-run institutions, created to address the impact of discrimination and exclusion, didn't discriminate in their admission policies. They were often little more than warehouses for any 'undesirable' sectors of society, an out-of-sight, out-of-mind solution to complex and multi-layered issues. These places were invariably built a discrete distance from polite society and housed countless individuals with intellectual disabilities.

It's easy, and perhaps convenient, to forget that these men and women were shunted aside by a society that was ill-equipped and unwilling to deal with them. Those that weren't institutionalized were often confined to their homes, seldom seen in public. Their lives were limited and sheltered; their growth stunted by the narrow perceptions of the times.

Many of their stories have been chronicled in recent years and while some of the goals and practices employed may have been well-intentioned – even considered enlightened – they were ultimately grounded in a model of segregation. A *Wholesome Horror: Poor Houses in Nova Scotia*, written by Brenda Thompson in 2018, chronicles life in these poor houses in graphic, sometimes heart-wrenching detail. Poor houses have traditionally been shrouded in mystery, marked by misery, and dismissed as the moral failings of a less enlightened time.

The existence of poorhouses and poor farms in Nova Scotia can be traced back all the way back to 1759, more than 100 years before Confederation. From the beginning, the inhabitants were a distillation of outcasts. By 1886, when the provincial government introduced municipal asylums for the express purpose of housing people with intellectual disabilities, the clientele remained diverse with a wide range of disabilities.

The stated goals were noble, if extremely patronizing: to offer care and rehabilitation in a safe environment. They were in fact a reaction to a collective public guilt and based more on pity than on any solid philosophical, medical, or scientific foundation. They claimed to offer 'moral treatment.' In other words, they believed that if the institutionalized were treated as normal human beings they would respond in kind and major behavioural changes would occur naturally. The tightly managed surroundings of an asylum would allow for optimum results with the ultimate objective of returning the individual to society.

On the surface that goal seems admirable, even progressive, but in reality the underlying motivation was to lessen the economic burden that this demographic placed on provincial coffers. In Nova Scotia, the philosophy also meant decentralization. Large provincial institutions located in Halifax were replaced by smaller, less expensive, county asylums.

To further ensure that municipal locations were cost effective, they were usually run as farms, making the residents unpaid farm labourers – in essence, slaves - and thereby subsidizing the enterprise. Those whose disabilities were less severe did most of the work. To compound the problem and belie the notion of "moral treatment," the people who oversaw the poor farms were often hired for their farming acumen and not for any qualifications based on expertise in care or support. The bottom line was cost; free labour ensured profitability, or at least self-sufficiency, and the Nova Scotia government benefitted. Despite a change in name and a misleading mission statement, the asylums remained little more than labour camps for the undesirables of the area, including those termed "the harmless insane."

Economics, in one form or other, continued to dictate practice well into the twentieth century. The intellectually challenged were seen as a burden on society and inevitably these people were devalued, both economically and socially. There are recorded instances of babies being born to mentally unstable mothers, and of these children being left to die if there were signs of Down syndrome or other various mental "defects."

The very thought that a time would come when these same devalued members of society would become masters of their own destinies and have an active voice in their own futures would have been considered ridiculous. Their futures were determined and limited by others. Their voices - if heard at all - were ignored or discounted.

To ensure that the asylums and farms remained productive, the criteria for residency was broadened. The list of eligible candidates grew to include the unmarried, the elderly, war veterans, the chronically ill, and as Thompson puts it, "stubborn children, beggars and fortune tellers." In short it was a catch-all, a solution to a plethora of problems, some real, some contrived.

Contributing to the misery of poor house residents was a belief first expressed by English philosopher and social reformer Jeremy Bentham. Although on most social issues he was an enlightened individual, that progressive streak did not extend to the treatment of the poor. He felt that the poor were naturally lazy and that poor houses merely facilitated and enabled that tendency. With that as his overriding thesis, he determined that poor houses should be as unpleasant as possible to discourage freeloaders. He further argued that the stigma attached to residents of poor houses was not only deserved but was, in fact, a good thing, a disincentive for people to go there.

His hope was that the poor house would become "an object of wholesome horror" so that those suffering financial hardship would choose to work, regardless of "how demeaning, degrading, or dangerous" their jobs were. Bentham got his wish; the stigma that he saw as an incentive to avoid the poor house was attached to all residents, regardless of their circumstance or reason for confinement. And once there, it was virtually impossible to be removed.

The flip side of that argument was expressed many decades later by Wolf Wolfensberger who suggested that institutions existed because their presence of these "unfortunates" among the population was threatening and distressing. His argument suggests that they represented the universal fear of frailty and vulnerability. Wolfensberger's theory seems to be borne out by the very fact that the standards for residency rapidly broadened to include various other classes of society's so-called undesirables.

Public attitudes often change with glacial speed and many of these notions persisted far into the 20th century. Poor houses were still a blight on the rural landscape of Nova Scotia in the 1960s and early 70s as perceptions continued to be shaped by ignorance and fear.

THE ANNAPOLIS VALLEY

The beautiful and bountiful Annapolis Valley was once home to more than a dozen poorhouses, including three in Kings County, at Billtown, Aylesford, and Horton (Greenwich). In 1922, these three crumbling facilities were closed and their "inmates" moved into a large and modern new building in Waterville known variously, and interchangeably, as the Waterville Poor House, the Kings County Home, the County Home, or the County Farm.

An article in the Wolfville Acadian newspaper of December, 1922 - reprinted in "A Wholesome Horror"– makes the new facility sound inviting, bordering on luxurious: "The new edifice is situated on elevated ground and commands a fine view of the surrounding country." It goes on to say, "The main floor has a large plaza on the south about 75" in length. Adjoining are the men's smoking-room, kitchen, dining room and recreation room on the east-end, with the apartments for the superintendents and officials in the wing at the same end. At the west end are similar rooms for women for sewing, recreation and dining rooms." The idyllic image no doubt conjured up by the readers of the day is destroyed in the final sentence of the article, "The basement is of concrete and is divided into furnace-rooms, work-shops, morgue, etc…"

The institution was renamed the Mountain View Home in 1964 and continued to house the same clientele until 1972, just two years after The Flower Cart first opened its doors, at which time it was transformed into a "shelter" for children with severe mental challenges.

Marlene Dodge worked at the Mountain View Home in the late 70s before embarking on a 40 year-career as head baker at The Flower Cart bakery. This experience makes her uniquely qualified to compare the old ways and the new. Her experience at Mountain View left an indelible mark and helped shape her views on working with the intellectually disabled. The memories of the time she spent there as a young woman are still fresh some forty years later.

"It was scary," she recalls. "Even seeing those places from a distance was eerie. You didn't even want to go past there. Mountain View was located on the outskirts of Waterville on county land. I believe that many in the general public at the time liked to hope it didn't exist but, in actual fact, a lot of people just didn't care. They chose a place on a hill. They were kept apart from society. There was a road in front of the building but the only people coming up and down that road were the staff coming to work and going home. No one cut across that property. It was just horrifying.

In the back of the building, there was a big field and we used to take people down there for a walk because it was really nice. We noticed some stones in one area so we thought that it must be the graveyard, but I didn't know until later that the whole field had people buried underneath. One time a man came to apply as janitor and he knew the history and told us about what had happened. They were outcasts and it makes you wonder what they died of....

Inside, the building had a strange aura. All those institutions sort of had that haunted feeling about them – a feeling of displacement, a certain smell, a certain atmosphere, a certain vibration as soon as you walked in the front door.

When I first started working there I didn't know what to expect because I'd never experienced institutions. Some people have family that they visit or somebody knows somebody who's there, but that was my first time in a place like that. My grandfather used to tell us stories about the old Greenwich poor house. It was a huge, scary old building and if a child died he would be taken away and you'd never see him again. He said they all had their own graveyard. That's all I knew when I arrived.

I'd never had any exposure in any way in my life to mentally handicapped people and Mountain View was an extremely diverse population with a huge variety of behaviours. There were people that couldn't live at home because they were physically dangerous - and believe me, they didn't need a weapon to harm someone. They were there because at home they might have attacked their sisters or parents or visitors, and they were just as dangerous to themselves.

A lot of the people there were medicated, especially the most serious cases, those that put other people in danger. There was always a nurse on duty and we had to report any extreme behaviour.

There were a lot of people who shouldn't have been there at all. I know because some of those people later ended up at The Flower Cart. I believe that some were there because their parents couldn't afford to feed them. So, then it becomes a nutritional issue and that in itself can definitely affect your mental stability and your self-esteem and everything.

You lived at home almost in neglect and then you're put in institutions. Some disabilities are obvious and others aren't, but Mountain View really was a catch-all. When we started to ask what exactly was wrong with an individual, you were often left wondering how they'd ended up in there. Why did parents send their children to these places? It could be a lack of money, of family support, of community support. That's a nasty thought, but it's true. Without these burdens, maybe most people would have made them a part of their home and done anything in their power to prevent that child from going to an institution."

I found it very inhumane. Everyone was brought down to a main area to eat. No one had a choice. Food was put on the table and if you couldn't feed yourself, someone would be quickly shoving it into your face so that the next sitting of people could come along. The dining space was large but it didn't house everyone. Staff were really eager to get people fed so that they could move the next crew in.

At that time in the early 1970s, there was a lot of uncertainty. There was so much in the media about downsizing institutions. Some people were very happy about that and some were not. The concern was about what would be done with the people that are that dangerous. There were some very aggressive people because the government pooled such a wide variety of residents. It didn't matter what the diagnosis was or the extent of the mental illness. If you needed a place, you went there, so there were some very aggressive people.

In late 70s they were in the process of arranging for the Mountain View building to be torn down. During the last segment of our placement we were told that those residents that wouldn't be going to go directly into a group home would be going into rehab. So they basically just pushed those people out.

Many weren't even from Kings County. And an effort was made to get people back to their own community. It was our job to take them there and make contact with their family. We'd call the family member to see if they'd like to meet their nephew or child. It was like, 'Here's your son. Tell him what you've been up to for the past 25 years.' It was our job to make that connection.

There was no stimulus at Mountain View. No people came in. We were completely cut off from the community. The building, it was all keyed. When you started, you were given main door keys, washroom keys, and keys for the six people's rooms that you were responsible for.

This was something that took me a while to learn. And those who had the realization that they were locked in knew the sound and meaning of every turn of every key. They knew if it was the staff. They knew if it was the laundry person coming to throw sheets on the bed. They knew the difference, and I always found that amazing. To think that the sound of keys had such significance for them. Only certain staff people might be allowed in to see certain residents. The head of the staff was allowed to go anywhere, but we had to get someone else to respond.

Our basic mandate was to care for the residents, keep them fed and warm and dry. That was it. Some of the residents had some money to take them bowling or do a few activities but that was only a certain few. There wasn't a whole lot of stimulation. There were a lot of disturbing things going on. People were tied by bed sheets to protect themselves and others. Some had physical disabilities. Those that weren't in a wheelchair would sometimes be wandering around and there were a lot of stairs. It was dangerous. Sometimes residents were wrapped in a sheet and tied up and watched through a hole in the door to see what they would do. At that time, the idea of these timeouts was pretty big. I refused to do that and I almost lost my job because of it. It wasn't exactly abusive but to me it felt inhumane.

After I'd had this experience, I thought I'd never want to work in an institution again. And then came the opportunity to work at The Flower Cart. The provincial government's goal was to lessen the number of institutions, although that wave had come around more than once. The Flower Cart was exactly what I wanted but I didn't even know it existed. It was an opportunity to work with people and teach them and improve their lives. I found it so appealing. It was a big eye-opener to me and quickly made me realize what I wanted to do as a young person."

In 1979, the old Waterville Poor House, now known as the Mountain View Home, was closed and later that same year, the structure was torn down, but Marlene's experiences there are seared into her memory. "It's was tragic when you think about it. I could understand why parents had to lie and say that person never existed. You could do that then and get away with it. Now the world is totally different."

The trend, begun in the early 70s, to close institutions and replace them with group homes and small option homes has been a major success story, notably in the Annapolis Valley. "In the early 1970s, with the closure of the Mountain View institution in Kings County, Nova Scotia was in the lead nationally in providing community supports to the most significantly disabled persons." said Dr. Michael Kendrick in his report from January 2001. "It is notable that...the number of people in Nova Scotia residential institutions has declined from 1200 in 1985 to slightly more than half as much."

KEITH STRONG, A PROFILE

It's one thing to talk in generalities about faceless residents of Nova Scotia's institutions for the intellectually disabled; it's quite another to see those individuals as real people and hear their personal stories. It's even more powerful when these former residents can contrast their institutional experiences with the more enlightened approaches that began in the 1970s. As a staff worker at Mountain View and The Flower Cart, Marlene Dodge is uniquely qualified to contrast the old ways with the new but as a client of both facilities, Keith Strong experienced the difference even more directly.

In 1955 Keith was born with Down syndrome. He was brought to the Mountain View Home at the age of four. He had been confined there his entire adult life until finally moved to a small group home as a grown man.

Although people had difficulty understanding his guttural, garbled speech, Keith had an engaging, outgoing personality and a warmth that overcame any lack of conventional communication skills. Marlene remembers him from her time as a staff worker at Mountain View and later as a participant at The Flower Cart.

"I knew Keith for many years so I could understand him where many couldn't. It wasn't so much his gestures as the sounds that he made. I knew when he was upset or happy or when he wanted to do something. He was very clever in the sense of being his own person. Hope was always his favourite word."

When Keith was 20 years old fate brought Jeff Moore to Mountain View. Jeff and his wife Debbie are social activists who would later start the Just Us! Coffee Roasters Co-Op. Before he met Keith, Jeff had previous summer job experience at a locked-ward psychiatric hospital and had been appalled at how inmates were treated. Now things were slowly starting to change and Debbie and Jeff were in the forefront of that change in the Valley.

Group homes were replacing large institutions and Jeff was working for the organization that was selecting people to place in those homes. The job inevitably led him to Mountain View and what would be a life-changing encounter for both Jeff and Keith. Immediately upon entering the aging facility, Moore was struck by the atmosphere of melancholy that permeated the place. Dreary, dark and sterile, the surroundings exuded a general impression of joylessness.

In the midst of this stark and oppressive setting appeared Keith Strong, brimming with confidence and good will. He welcomed Moore with open arms, literally. It was quickly apparent that Keith did not belong in such a place. Keith invited him and his close friend John MacNeil to take up residence at a group home nearby.

It wasn't long before Keith moved in with Jeff and Debbie at their home in Wolfville where he settled in and he lived with them as a de facto member of the family. The person who had spent most of his life in a cold, impersonal institution finally knew the intimacy of a close-knit family. The Moore's daughters treated him like a brother, encouraging him in any way they could. "They took him to Ottawa" recalls Marlene, who became a friend of the Moores. "They included him in everything they did. Through them, he was able to communicate with many people including politicians that he'd encounter and he always brought up the subject of hope. Whenever he spoke with others he used that word."

The Moores also had a child with Down syndrome named Gregory and in 1981, they, along with Keith Strong and his friend John founded the L'Arche Homefires community in the Valley. Keith was the first person to take up residence in the original home. There were no day programs at that time at L'Arche so Keith attended the Flower Cart where he was reunited with Marlene Dodge. Debbie Moore and The Flower Cart founder Jean DeWolfe became friends. They encouraged the bond between Keith and Jean's daughter, Linda, who also had Down syndrome. The two friends worked together at The Flower Cart bakery.

"Keith was quite a guy," former executive director Joanne Porter recalls. "He was there when I started as director, working in the bakery. Keith knew what he wanted. I remember one day I was told to go down to the bakery and speak with him because he had decided that he wanted to do the work his way. He really expressed his opinion. He was very vocal but not verbal, but he had all the intonations of verbalizing.

"I was firm with him and told him that the job had to be done our way, not his. I left through the doorway and was on the steps and I stopped to do something, and I heard him say 'Old cow!'. I thought, 'Ok, first of all, he's venting and now he'll get back to work. Second of all, he waited until I got through the door, and third, if I hadn't paused on the stairs, I wouldn't even have heard it. So, I figured those were really good social skills and I didn't call him on it at all."

Marlene watched Keith's progress with pride and when he passed away she took solace in knowing he'd been able to experience a full and productive life, accomplishing things that no one would have ever imagined he could. There were no more clattering keys and no more locked doors. Fittingly, his memorial service was a celebration of life, and hope.

CHAPTER TWO: THE VISION AND THE VISIONARY

Prior to 1970, before Jean DeWolfe, an entire population of intellectually handicapped people was without a support system of any kind, save for family. Long before the words of The Flower Cart's first mission statement were committed to paper they were an idea which became a vision. The Flower Cart exists because of that vision and it is a practical response to a very real need. This underlying belief system still informs every decision that is made there.

THE VISION

Most landmarks are, by definition, well-known and their relevance appreciated yet despite dedicated efforts to educate the public and the undeniable impact it continues to have on the Valley's business and social life, The Flower Cart remains something of an enigma to much of the population. We can clearly see that it's a hive of activity with people coming and going throughout the week but few know the extent of its reach or the impact it has in our daily lives.

Fittingly, the weathered building that has been the home of The Flower Cart began its existence as New Minas Elementary School, a place of learning, and has maintained that noble course ever since. After it had served its original purpose, it briefly became part of The Little Red Schoolhouse Program, before it was purchased and re-purposed as the new home for The Flower Cart.

Unimposing and relatively accessible, it bears no physical resemblance to its ugly predecessors, the poor houses and other institutions described previously, and unlike those foreboding, isolated places, it sits in the social mainstream of the Annapolis Valley, an easy nine-iron shot from the KenWo Golf and Country Club, and across the street from Evangeline Middle School.

Annapolis Valley businesses certainly know about The Flower Cart. Those companies with the foresight to employ Flower Cart participants have benefitted financially through improved productivity. Companies like Michelin, Just Us! Coffee Roasters Co-Op, and dozens of others continue to make use of the capabilities and work ethic that their Flower Cart employees bring to the job every day. It has been proven, time and time again, that hiring workers with the special skills they have acquired from Flower Cart programs makes good business sense.

Quite possibly The Flower Cart has become so much a part of our lives that we take it for granted. We have limited awareness of its history, its purpose, or the extent of its impact on the community. In reality, we encounter and support that purpose every day when we buy bread, purchase tires, stop for a coffee, or engage in countless other daily activities.

We are left with the vague notion that something good is happening behind those walls and are content to leave it at that. In some ways, that's a good thing because it means that the participants who make use of this extraordinary place have been seamlessly accepted and welcomed as productive members of the community. On the flip side, this lack of awareness prevents many from appreciating and celebrating one of Nova Scotia's most inspiring and hard-won success stories.

The Flower Cart has adapted to keep pace with societal shifts and marketplace needs. Not surprisingly, this dynamic of change-on-change periodically brings about something akin to an identity crisis within the organization. The continual state of flux within this micro environment mirrors changes in the wider community.

The one constant is the vision. When looked at with the benefit of hindsight, the original goals of the founders seem modest, but given the context of the time they were established, they are anything but. They were, in fact, quite radical by contemporary standards.

On September 8, 1970, after two frenetic years of planning and preparation, The Flower Cart opened its doors. Its stated purpose was to address the needs of "mentally handicapped young adults." It was not started to bring about systemic change. The Flower Cart began as a very personal quest by a mother to make her daughter's life richer and more productive.

That's why the history of The Flower Cart can't be told in statistics or spreadsheets or even in the yellowing annual general reports that record particulars of each successive year of its existence. It can only be told in the lasting impact it has made on the lives of real people.

JEAN DEWOLFE, A PROFILE

"There were few options in pre-1970 Nova Scotia. The schools were working hard to provide meaningful programming and talking to older resource teachers, but it was really discouraging. When the kids graduated they just fell into a void. Parents didn't know what to do. And that was the motivating factor for Jean DeWolfe. Linda wasn't going to do that."

— Joanne Porter, former executive director and neighbour of the DeWolfe family

Jean Francis Ross was born in 1923 and grew up as an only child on a small farm in Weston, Kings County, Nova Scotia. After completing her public schooling, she moved up the Valley to Wolfville where she attended Horton Academy for three years from 1941-1944, graduating with a Diploma in Secretarial Science. It was while employed as a secretary that she met and subsequently married Owen DeWolfe, a successful Wolfville businessman and owner of

R.W. DeWolfe, growers and exporters of Medford Brand Annapolis Valley Apples.

Owen was a descendant of the same DeWolfes that had given the university town its name, and the quiet, unassuming former air force pilot had a stellar record of community service. He had served as chair of Eastern Kings Memorial Hospital and as a member of town council, and was president of the Wolfville branch of the Royal Canadian Legion. As a member of St. Andrew's United Church, he was a tireless fundraiser for a wide range of charitable organizations.

Jean and Owen soon became a team to be reckoned with within the Valley community. While assisting her husband with his burgeoning business, Jean became an active member of Wolfville society. Friendly, social, and energetic, she attracted a circle of friends from various walks of life. She was an avid golfer and dedicated member of St. Andrew's United Church, singing in the choir and working with the United Church Women on worthwhile causes. Among the causes that she championed were the CNIB, Special Olympics, and the Ken-Wo Golf and Country Club.

Jean and Owen had four children, Ross, Linda, Emily, and Suzanne. Linda was born with Down syndrome, a diagnosis that wasn't made until she was 18 months old. The news, delivered by "an unsympathetic physician," was devastating. The dire circumstance was compounded with the realization that there was nowhere to turn for help.

"I'd never had anything to do with handicapped people," Jean told Wendy Elliott of *The Advertiser* in 1992. "Institutions were the norm," she recalled. The severely handicapped had no right to liberty or justice, back then.

The subject of Linda's Down syndrome was studiously avoided by many as not being a fit topic for polite company. Although supportive, close friends avoided confronting the obvious. Even the family doctor could offer little concrete advice for the DeWolfe family. "There was nothing at that time for kids with Down syndrome in the Valley," recalls Ross DeWolfe, the eldest of the DeWolfe children. Like other families in this circumstance, they were left to cope as best they could. Ross remembers his mother's selfless dedication to Linda. "Linda and our mother were really close," he says. "She was her life and she took all of her time."

Jean and Owen were an indomitable force in the lives of all their children and Jean quickly determined that her daughter would be given every opportunity to live a full and productive life. She didn't care about any social shame that might have been attached to having an intellectually disabled child. Quite the opposite, her daughter's condition only served to deepen her commitment to social activism and she became a life-long champion of people with intellectual disabilities. Nevertheless, Joanne Porter recalls the efforts made by Linda's parents to shelter and protect her.

"Jean did realize that there was a stigma that Linda would carry. And people would be quicker to judge than with her other children, so Emily could go out with ripped jeans or a dirty t-shirt and people would just think she'd been out playing. Linda she always felt had to go that extra step to look good."

Linda's development was slow. She didn't begin walking until the age of four but younger sisters Emily and Susanne were happy to encourage her and pass along their skills. In fact, despite the lack of physical or speech therapy, Wolfville was one of the more enlightened and accepting communities in Nova Scotia, and friends and neighbours embraced the engaging young girl. She attended regular nursery school, primary, and grade one, but after that there were no appropriate special education classes suited to her needs. "There was nothing for her here and they just wouldn't teach her in Wolfville School at that time," says her sister Emily.

The DeWolfe's explored the limited options and, after much soul searching, decided that the best choice for Linda, albeit a painful one, was to send her away to the Nova Scotia Youth Training Centre in Truro, a residential facility for children with intellectual disabilities. "Linda didn't cry about going away to Truro," recalls Porter.

For the next decade, she would spend several months of each year in this residential school. Her parents made the almost four-hour return trip to visit her as often as possible. "Owen was well connected and well respected in the community," says Porter. "He would go up to Truro every month, always on a Sunday. His daughter was there and he was darn well going to visit her. They'd go out for dinner. It was a ritual and it didn't seem to have any negative consequences.

"That was a big trip on the number one highway. I went with them a couple of times and I found it very difficult. Linda was a different person there. I remember being quite annoyed with the teacher and the way she spoke to Linda. I was Linda's age and the teacher was very directive.

Emily, 61, the DeWolfe's second daughter, holds vivid recollections of her big sister. "Linda was a beautiful little girl," she says. "She had to leave Wolfville as a seven-year old to go to school in another town, hours away. That's heartbreaking. I never really talked to mom about how hard that must have been for her and our father - to have to send their little girl away to live because they had no other choice. We drove up to visit her regularly and she came home probably once a month but it still must have been horrible - really, really hard. She attended the Truro school from September to June from the age of seven until she was eighteen because there was nothing else.

"Linda would come home for Christmas vacation and for Easter and other holidays, and she'd be home for the summer, and then go back up. My husband and I were in Truro recently and we drove by that big red and white water tower right beside the training centre. It brought back memories of when we used to drive Linda back there. Whenever I saw that water tower, I knew that Linda's school was next door and that we'd be leaving her there. I like to think it was not all dark. Linda seemed to like it when she was there and I know there were people that Linda really liked there, and my parents were certainly in touch with them a lot... but it was just not normal.

"I was too little to really know what was going on. It was just the way it was, and we never questioned her going there. I'm sure my mother probably had some teary moments, and I'm sure that anyone with kids of their own can't even imagine how you'd send a 7-year old away. She was just so beautiful - beautiful looking and beautiful inside and out."

Emily suggests that these excruciating periods of separation were what motivated Jean to take action. "Having been through that, Mom probably decided that 'When she gets home for good I'm going to get something going for her' because there was nothing. That's the thing, you brought her home and then what?" That day finally arrived when Linda reached the age of 18 and was no longer eligible to attend the Truro centre. The joy in bringing their daughter home was tempered by the knowledge that unless things changed, she was would be facing a bleak future.

"After finishing her years in Truro she would have had to stay at home for the rest of her life," says her brother Ross. "But our mother was a determined woman and she had a lot of connections. She was always able to make quite a lot out of nothing."

It wasn't in Jean to give up. One of her friends, Carol Armstrong, a child psychologist at the Fundy Mental Health Centre, suggested that a sheltered workshop setting might be an ideal solution. Sheltered workshops were growing in popularity in the United States but hadn't yet spread north of the border and certainly not to Nova Scotia. These workshops would soon become a key component in addressing the needs of intellectually disabled individuals across Canada.

The idea was to provide work training and even employment for adults who otherwise would be deemed unemployable. That group included those with various physical or intellectual disabilities. The workshop system had undergone a transformation from its previous incarnation. These sheltered workshops represented the leading edge, a vehicle for changing attitudes and providing meaningful employment.

The conversation with Carol Armstrong sparked a glimmer of hope in Jean DeWolfe and the idea that had been planted continued to grow and take shape. It was nourished by discussions with Owen and shaped over coffee with her circle of friends, many of whom were mental health professionals and committed to the cause. Her eclectic group included Joanne Porter, Carmela Enzinas, Lorraine Boland, Carol Armstrong, and Lois Schrag, all of whom would become key partners in the birth of The Flower Cart. Their encouragement inspired her to act.

Although she was too young to remember many details about the beginnings of The Flower Cart, Emily recalls the generosity and passion of her parents. "I'm sure Dad was the moneybags behind a lot of it," she says. "I know he was very generous with the finances because he was always generous and loved Linda. But Mom would certainly have been the voice behind everything." After researching the topic thoroughly, Owen and Jean proposed the establishment of a sheltered workshop for mentally handicapped persons. It was the genesis of The Flower Cart. What began as a very personal goal quickly grew to positively impact all disabled adults in the area.

Carmela Enzinas, later to become the chairperson of The Flower Cart's initial board, credits Jean's determination, perseverance, and pragmatism for what followed. "Jean knew that after the Youth Training Centre, there was no place for a Down syndrome adult like Linda to go. That was the big impetus for starting The Flower Cart. The DeWolfe's were political people and had political connections in government circles. Jean met with people in Halifax and that's how we got our first grant, which was wonderful. The Lion's Club and other service clubs were also wonderful. It really does take a village."

There were practical considerations as well, says Emily. "Mom really liked to be out and about. She was a very social person, not one to sit at home with an adult child. That wasn't what she wanted to do and she definitely didn't want that for Linda - to be sitting at home doing nothing. Because of those two things, she thought, I've got to get something going for Linda here, and she did."

Linda was no shrinking violet either, having inherited her mother's independent streak. Even before The Flower Cart, she swam regularly at the Acadia pool and was a well-known presence around town. She even participated in the Special Olympics.

Jean discovered that there were two other girls like Linda in the immediate area and made contact with their parents. She even went so far as to personally scout out a location for a sheltered workshop – the vacant former elementary school. She launched an ambitious letter writing campaign across Canada, explained the sheltered workshop concept and solicited help for the barely embryonic plan that was starting to consume her. "The Flower Cart became a cause that was near and dear to her," says Ross. It wasn't long before her efforts began to generate support in the form of financial donations.

The challenge was to turn her vision into brick and mortar reality. An array of challenges lay in her path, not least of which was staffing. Jean had numerous connections at the university and in town and she used them all. "We drew people in one by one," she told Wendy Elliott.

Initial expectations were modest by today's standards but almost radical by the prevailing attitudes of the day. It was necessary to educate the public, especially those families with intellectually disabled young adults. At that time, many candidates for the school were kept at home, Jean recalled. "They couldn't comb their own hair. They'd no leeway to develop." She wanted so much more for Linda. She wanted to make her daughter's life, and the lives of other attendees, more interesting, more hopeful, more challenging, and as normal as possible. The notion of working and making money wasn't yet a priority. "The point was to give them good days and something to look forward to," she said.

Despite Jean's extraordinary efforts and the obvious need, people weren't exactly lined up to take advantage of the new facility when the doors opened in 1970. "When we started we had a hard time finding four people to participate," recalls Carmela Enzinas.

"Parents were reluctant. It was hard to get their kids out of the house. There was a combination of embarrassment and protectiveness."

Now, fifty years after her mother's dream was realized and The Flower Cart first opened its doors, Emily considers the impact it had on her older sister. "She was at The Flower Cart for a long time and the influence on her was huge," she says. "It certainly helped to make her more independent. I remember she'd take the bus out and the bus back. When Linda was there, she worked in the bakery a lot – the Baker's Dozen. She even worked at Tim Horton's in Wolfville after leaving The Flower Cart. It produced a big change in her and developed her personality and self-confidence. Linda had quite a following, a lot of fans in this part of the Valley."

"Imagine if she'd just been sitting at home without all that stimulation. All the social interaction was key to her development. That's what she and other intellectually disabled adults really need, to be in the community, not locked away somewhere by themselves. I think she was really fortunate in her life and I think The Flower Cart had a lot to do with that."

Emily realizes that Linda was also extremely fortunate in her place of birth and in having parents like Owen and Jean. "We were so lucky to live in Wolfville," she said. "We were lucky to have Linda because she was really, really special but she was lucky to have us, too. Mom and Dad could give her whatever she wanted, and I think Wolfville was very accepting of her. My parents knew a lot of people – many were influential people – and they liked Linda and took her under their wings."

Jean DeWolfe lived to see her vision realized to an extent that she and her small band of community activists couldn't have imagined in 1970. The vision continues to be followed and expanded years after her death. Because of her, participants in the various Flower Cart programs not only live interesting lives, but productive and fulfilling lives in which they are respected and valued. Almost certainly the original vision didn't encompass the notion that participants would be fairly remunerated for the work they do or that they would have a say in their own development. Twenty-two years after they opened the doors, Mrs. DeWolfe was happy to see that happening but even more pleased to observe of her creation, "They [The Flower Cart] never put making money ahead of individuals."

Long after her time at The Flower Cart, Linda continued to be a familiar figure in the town of Wolfville. She loved being out in the community, working and making new friends. As she aged, she developed Alzheimer's and dementia (which often happens to those with Down syndrome) and died at the the age of 55.

When Jean DeWolfe passed away at the age of 89 in 2012, then executive director Roger Tatlock borrowed a quotation from renowned cultural anthropologist Margaret Mead to pay her tribute. "'Never doubt that a small group of thoughtful, committed citizens can change the world. Indeed, it is the only thing that ever has.'" To which Tatlock added, "I offer that each of these groups needs a leader. Mrs. DeWolfe was such a leader."

EMILY DEWOLFE, A PROFILE

The Flower Cart will always be considered Jean DeWolfe's greatest legacy, and a legacy that was passed on to the next DeWolfe generation. Jean's daughter, Emily DeWolfe, had an intimate knowledge of the challenges and rewards associated with raising an intellectually disabled person. Although she was too young to remember much about the actual opening of The Flower Cart, the organization became a part of the family vocabulary throughout her adolescence and into adulthood. The connection informed the future direction of her own working life.

"After I got my first degree from Acadia in the spring of 1979, I spent the summer working at The Flower Cart and I liked it a lot. I worked with some interesting people and enjoyed watching them grow. It was a very rewarding experience. I thought that's what I'd do with my life – work with mentally challenged adults. I decided to go back to Acadia to pursue a twelve-month B.Ed. course in special education. I graduated in 1980 and started teaching special education. I especially enjoyed the years when I was with more severely learning-disabled kids. We just had some really fun times together. It was rewarding and there was never a dull moment. I'm sure it was because of Linda that I chose special education. When you grow up with that, it becomes part of you."

CHAPTER THREE: THE FIRST DECADE

On September 8, 1970, after more than a year of planning and fundraising by Jean DeWolfe and her friends, the Flower Cart opened its doors to four young adult women with intellectual disabilities. The former New Minas Elementary School had been acquired on a rent-free basis from the Kings County Amalgamated School Board as the premises for their sheltered workshop. Renovations and installation of furnishings would continue at the site until Christmas.

During its first year of operation, the administration of the Flower Cart Activity-Training Centre (the name would be changed to the more accurate Flower Cart Sheltered Workshop in the spring of 1971) fell to the Management Committee that was responsible to the Canadian Association for the Mentally Retarded (CAMR). The program operated under the sponsorship of the Kings County branch of CAMR. Financial responsibility was split between the association, the community, and the Department of Public Welfare through the Canada Assistance Plan. The 7-person committee, made up of community volunteers, issued its first report for the period of September 1970 to September 1971.

Each committee member brought something different and valuable to the table. The Executive consisted of social worker Carmella Enzinas, Chairman; Lorraine Bolland, Treasurer; Jean DeWolfe, Secretary; and Lois Schrag, Program Coordinator. Also on the committee were vice-chairman Ray Hubley and psychologist Carol Armstrong of the Fundy Mental Health Clinic, who also did the testing of participants and oversaw admissions. So far, the administrators out-numbered the number of participants.

Schrag was the only staff member, serving dual roles as instructor and program coordinator. When boys were added to the mix in early 1971, Bob Mills was hired as a second instructor and Boys Program Coordinator.

Despite the obvious need for such a facility, people weren't exactly lined up to make use of the innovative new workshop when it opened its doors. "When we started we had a hard time finding four people to participate," says Enzinas. "Parents were reluctant. It was hard to get their kids out of the house. There was embarrassment and protectiveness."

The school board provided transportation. Kentville Lions were very helpful. The original enrollment consisted of four females, but four males had been added before the end of the school year.

During the early-70s move toward de-institutionalization, the Nova Scotia government was searching for ways to transition to a new model. "The Department of Community Services and minister Edmund Morris really appreciated what was going on with us," recalls Enzinas. "They became very collaborative, and soon standards and policy were introduced."

The origin of the name Flower Cart is the subject of some mild dispute. Former director, Joanne Porter believes it may have been a holdover from the "age of Aquarius" decade that was just ending. "Hey, it was the 1960s," she says with a barely discernable eye roll. "Everything was flowers. Flower power. It was also about providing the right conditions for students to bloom, I suppose."

The Flower Cart was breaking new ground and the Management Committee was forced to learn on the fly and adapt quickly to unforeseen developments. Despite the creative chaos, a sense of humour seems to have been maintained. A hand-written note tucked inside the First Annual Report file folder suggested, "It has been said

that a committee constitutes the unwilling appointing the unquali-
fied to do the unnecessary."

The first few years of The Flower Cart were rife with challenges. Some were inevitable growing pains, others threatened to de-
rail the vision. They were all part of a steep learning curve for everyone involved - administrators, staff, and participants. Change was the
only constant. Change of staff, change of board members, change of
programs. Somehow, during a period of constant evolution, personnel turnover, and identity development, there was progress, and
while they were baby steps compared to what was to follow, they
were major strides in the history of The Flower Cart.

Highlights of the initial year of operation included the rent-
free acquisition of the former New Minas Elementary School from the
Kings County Amalgamated School Board as well as a successful financial campaign that allowed for needed renovations and installation of furnishings and equipment.

The initial enrollment of four girls were under the guidance
of Mrs. Schrag and their first task was to work with the committee to
prepare for the official opening on November 27. It was a big event,
with more than 200 people in attendance. Mills was hired as a coordinator and instructor in January and two boys were added to the
program in March of 1971 when half of the basement was converted
into a woodworking shop.

Fire insurance and liability coverage were attained with
money from donations and the remaining $8000 was invested. A
grant of $5000 was received from the Department of Public Welfare.

An admissions committee was formed to assess applicants to
The Flower Cart and decide who was eligible to attend. The basic criteria were the ability to function in a sheltered workshop environment and the ability to travel alone on buses or in taxis. "We enrol
those in the high-trainable and educable range," the report stated.
Since the school board had declared that the admission of "mentally
retarded" pupils would continue within the system until age eighteen, it was determined that would be the age for admission to The

Flower Cart. The report added, "We foresee a continuing increased demand for this program," predicting the application of approximately five trainees per year.

The initial program consisted of a five-day week that ran from 9:00 am to 3:00 pm, allowing trainees to use the school board bus system. The Flower Cart year mirrored the school year for this reason, although the long-term goal was to make it a year-long operation.

The first expressed goal of The Flower Cart Sheltered Workshop, as stated by the Management Committee in the first annual report was "basically that of helping each young person develop and function to the full extent of his or her abilities." The design of the first year was aimed at furthering that goal. "To achieve this goal, we have tried to offer a program of evolving methods of exposure, training, and experience to help them cope more adequately with the various requirements of production, the family and the community." The program included the making of handcrafts – for the girls this meant hand- and machine-sewing and embroidery, braiding, knitting, cutting, and folding. They also learned the various aspects of preparing and serving meals.

Meanwhile the boys were taught the basics of sanding and varnishing along with an introduction to simple woodworking tools. They also took over the duties of weeding, cutting grass and shoveling snow at the facility, skills that might offer them employment opportunities in the community and lowered maintenance costs.

All trainees were also taught to answer the phone, prepare the morning break, clean up after lunch, and look after the pet gerbils and plants. Personal hygiene and conduct were also emphasized. Shopping trips were made on a regular basis to increase self confidence in interacting with the public.

The first year also saw the beginning of the contract and sub-contract work that would one day become the financial backbone of the organization. At the time, the jobs were a key means of fulfilling the stated mandate of allowing participants to reach their potential. There was no suggestion that it would, or could, play a major role in

The Flower Cart's long-term viability. It was, however, a first step in the long road to self-reliance.

The participants packaged "Flowers of Hope" Seeds and folded maps for the Kentville Advertiser. It was a modest start but one that not only motivated the trainees but offered encouragement and validation to the small group of administrators who were watching their dream slowly come true.

In that initial year of operation, the boys' first project was to build a canteen for the Apple Blossom Festival. The effort won them first prize. They also labelled and painted litter barrels for the annual event. Placing The Flower Cart name on the containers was one of the first efforts to introduce the new organization to the Valley.

The social growth of trainees was always a priority. Parties were organized by various community and school groups. There were outings, restaurant visits, trips to the beach, and a variety of outdoor activities.

Before the first fiscal year (September 1970-August 1971) was even in the books, a decision was made that The Flower Cart Activity-Training Centre would be henceforth be known as The Flower Cart Sheltered Workshop. The Flower Cart had not only survived their first year, they also had shown the kind of adaptability and tenacity that figured well for the future. Turning an idea into reality is no easy task and requires the diverse talents of many people working toward a common goal.

The financial statement for The Flower Cart's first year of operation begins with the reassuring words, "It has been a most successful year financially..." Accountant George L. Doane, who donated the services of his firm to audit the books and produce the financial statement, went on to say that the community had responded generously to a campaign requesting donations for initial capital expenses.

Public interest in the new venture was high thanks largely to the stellar efforts of Management Committee members who spoke to more than two dozen community groups, including churches, service clubs, and schools. Some community groups even held occasional meetings at The Flower Cart to see first-hand what they were all about. Local media provided generous coverage of happenings at the new enterprise. The enhanced public profile led to grants from the Town of Wolfville, the Town of Kentville and the Municipality of Kings. Acadia University offered up its pool for trainees once a week and students in various fields of study volunteered their time and expertise for supervision and instruction. Valley Lanes Bowling reserved lanes for weekly participant outings and the Wolfville skating rink followed suit. The entire community - individuals and organizations - seemed to embrace The Flower Cart. The challenge would be to maintain this level of interest, enthusiasm, and financial support.

Although 50% of the net operating cost was reimbursed to the sheltered workshop by the Province of Nova Scotia through the Canada Assistance Act, that left another 50% to be raised from other sources and endeavours. As the committee looked back over the year with satisfaction, they also pondered their future and the funding needed to make their plans a reality.

The idea of a full-time administrator was proposed, someone to coordinate a sustainable and consistent cash flow. "We need to secure means of financial solvency that would not be dependent entirely on charitable donations", said a spokesman for the Canadian Association for the Mentally Retarded (CAMR).

Success is a double-edged sword and with enrollment expected to double in the next year and continue to grow at an increased rate, new and better facilities would be needed to accommodate their activities. It was decided that stipends were to be paid to trainees and this cost had to be offset. New and larger sub-contracts were a must if The Flower Cart was to survive and prosper.

It was decided to restructure the Management Board into two committees, one to look after administration and management concerns and another with programme responsibilities. With the enrolment now at 11 - six females and five males — structural changes were on the horizon. The new coordinator of the women's program, Pam Brown, resigned at the end of the year to be replaced by Anne Malyon, who had volunteered with the programme the previous year.

With a successful first year under their belt, The Flower Cart team began their second full year with renewed energy and a sense of guarded optimism. Mrs. Pamela Brown joined Bob Mills as the new instructor, replacing Lois Schrag, and the administrative structure underwent changes designed to make it more responsive to the needs of the growing enterprise.

In May of 1972, Charlotte Haley, Jack Buntain, Bill Wade, John Hawkins, Mr. E.W. Peill, and Bernard Mason were added to the original management board. It was decided that effective September 1972, two committees would be formed, one to address administrative and management concerns and one to look after programme responsibilities. By-laws were drawn up in committee and debated but the board felt that they would prefer to maintain an informal structure and the by-laws were tabled until a later date.

Year two brought encouraging signs of progress as staff reported trainees' improvement in socializing, self-confidence, ability to concentrate, and acceptance of responsibility, as well as the mastering of specific new skills. There was also a need to develop a more specific and progressive programme.

A sub-contract for packaging Bingo cards for the Lion's Club proved very successful and whetted the appetite for similar types of contracts. The expanded board was expected to kickstart a more aggressive search for such opportunities. Board Chairman Carmela Enzinas reported that financial support came from a variety of service clubs and churches in the area, as well as from private individuals.

The 50% funding through the Canada Assistance Act represented the only guaranteed annual support for The Flower Cart, a fact of great concern to the board. The Flower Cart enrollment had increased and with it the need for additional staff, as well as a workshop manager and possibly even an executive director. The balance sheet for the second year of operation showed revenues of $13,616.97 (including $4,391 from the Province of NS grant and roughly $5,000 in donations from various sources) and liabilities of $11, 862. 93 (the largest chunk being salaries of $4,322) leaving a balance of $1,754.04.

In the spring of 1973, The Flower Cart sought to be incorporated as a body separate from CAMR because of "the exigencies of various aspects of liability." Their efforts met with initial resistance from the CAMR but by August all documents related to The Flower Cart included the new designation. They were now The Flower Cart Incorporated Activity Training Centre, "an autonomous organization sponsored by the CAMR." Despite the changes, the relationship between the two groups remained strong. The incorporated body had a 15-member board of directors representing business, education, and employment, as well as social service professionals from Kings County.

In the early years The Flower Cart was still struggling to define itself. The identity crisis was understandable. Vision and practicality are two different things and it often takes time to consolidate the two. This passage from the Chairman's annual report suggests a focus on growth and responsibility:

"The program is designed to present a happy environment in which to learn and work. The development of ordinary living skills, acceptable social behaviour, and personal hygiene habits are basic to the functioning of the individuals. Simple handicrafts, the use of small tools, the preparation of meals, and household cleaning operations are part of the daily activities."

From this assessment of the current reality, the Chairman's report pivots to talk about what The Flower Cart could become. It would be impossible not to hear the passion, tinged with frustration, in the closing statement from chairman Charlotte Haley: "So The Flower Cart needs an ongoing project, and there is a real need for a small sheltered industry and/or farm training program. Problems of workmanship and volume can be overcome; handicaps and hang-ups can be eased. There is concern for trainees working in on-the-job training, and then full time in the labour force, since some job experiments have not proved too successful. Thus there is a step by step process possible for the trainees. The Flower Cart is only one aspect of what can be done to help the mentally retarded."

The Fourth Annual Report was blunt in its conclusions. "An activity training centre is neither a sheltered workshop nor a social hideout for the trainees," wrote Haley. "It is not realistic to assume that the trainees are willing to participate in a program which does not provide new and varied levels of challenge for each individual as he or she develops."

In the spring of 1974, executive director Anne Malyon provided a year's end status report that reflected the growing pains which are a natural by-product of development and progress. Programming was singled out for attention. "A number of the trainees have been at the Centre for several years and as they develop there is a need for the programme to develop in response," she wrote. Sub-contracts provided stability and satisfaction for the trainees and allowed the staff to do more one-on-one work, but such contract work was sporadic. This resulted in slow and uneven programme development.

Malyon emphasized the need for a sheltered industry or more regular contract work as a base for the overall programme. She went on to say that "the need for a sheltered industry or regular contract work as a strong base for the overall programme is essential and should be a priority in future planning."

Also during the 1973-74 school year, the former elementary school that housed The Flower Cart was given a major make-over, painted inside and out "improving the atmosphere immensely." In addition to cosmetic changes, alterations of a more substantive nature were also called for. A manual of Policies and Procedures was drawn up and accepted as the general guidelines for both staff and the board.

ANNE MALYON, A PROFILE

In 1973, Anne Malyon became the first Executive Director of The Flower Cart. She began her directorship by addressing the need for programme changes. With the guidance of Program Chairman Lorraine Boland, she set out to enact the changes that the management team had deemed necessary. Their efforts met with mixed results. While sub-contracts obtained in the first part of the year succeeded in providing, "a stable, satisfying and enjoyable programme for the trainees and gave the staff greater freedom to work on an individual basis with trainees", many of these contracts dried up in the second half and programme development slowed as a result.

Work experience for participants in on-the-job training, followed by full-time work showed mixed results at best. While those trainees who spent short periods in work situations coped well with the actual work, it was found that they required more "support and encouragement in adjusting to the new demands being placed on them."

It was a valiant first effort and underlined the need to deliver appropriate levels of programming to accommodate each individual. The diversity and range of intellectual disabilities made this a challenge. To this end, it was decided that more consistent contract work was needed.

There were other significant developments during Malyon's first year. For the first time, stipends of 25 cents per day were paid to give trainees experience in handling money. While the amount was modest, this practice would set an important precedent for what would follow over the intervening years.

The Board of Management developed a Manual of Policies and Procedures for the general guidance of the staff and the Board. Change was a constant. As with most start-up enterprises, The Flower Cart continued to struggle with personnel loses at both the board and staff levels. The make-up of the Board of Management underwent numerous changes as responsibilities were reallocated or redefined.

To encourage greater continuity, it was decided that board members would serve a three-year term.

As she settled into her leadership role, Malyon did her best to ensure that her staff was kept current on the latest research. Employees attended training sessions throughout the Maritimes and in-service training opportunities increased as the "vast reservoir of expertise" available in Kings County was identified and utilized. Staff was able to attend conferences featuring Wolf Wolfensburger, Mark Gold, and other pioneers in the development of progressive programs for those with intellectual disabilities.

THE ONLY CONSTANT IS CHANGE

As the decade approached the halfway point, change seemed to be the only constant as the list of programs continued to expand and the staff grew. In fact, in the early years of The Flower Cart the staff as well as the management committee itself was in a constant state of flux with positions changing, people leaving, and others entering to replace them.

The provincial Department of Social Services, through the Canada Assistance Act, announced that the amount paid to sheltered workshops would be raised from 50% to 65% of operating costs. This made possible renovations and redecoration of the building, including the development of a safe recreation area.

As the decade reached the halfway mark, The Flower Cart was showing more confidence, defining themselves and building momentum. Enrollment reached 25 full-time participants in 1975. That same year one of The Flower Cart's most defining and successful commercial ventures began, a seamless partnering of training and commerce. The opening of a bakery, initially known as The Baker's Dozen signalled a transition from handicraft activities to programs that were more in tune with local business needs. Since then, the smell of freshly baked bread and other delicious temptations have drawn thousands of Annapolis Valley people to buy a variety of baked goods.

A committee led by Lorraine Boland brought the bakery initiative to fruition with the help of a $22,500 Local Initiatives Program grant. With a 1975-76 budget of $35,000, of which 35% had to come from non-government sources, the grant was crucial. Despite initial challenges and setbacks, it would soon become one of The Flower Cart's defining features and one of its most successful enterprises.

Several trainees had worked for local employers throughout the year with mixed success and it soon became apparent that additional training within The Flower Cart was needed. The Baker's Dozen work-training unit would meet the needs of those trainees and provide opportunities for real-world work experiences.

Malyon ended her time as executive director during the 1976-77 year and assumed the programming portfolio. Macha MacKay led the organization briefly until August of 1977, when Jonanne Porter was hired.

Once again The Flower Cart underwent a name change. Effective June 10, 1976 it was to be the New Minas Adult Training Centre. This name was slow to catch on in the community and proved to be short-lived, for by the fall of 1977 it was once again The Flower Cart.

HALF A DECADE

Success doesn't come without challenges and the mid-seventies were a period of growth, change, and expansion at The Flower Cart. The one constant was the support of the local community and especially the various service clubs in the Wolfville-Kentville corridor.

In 1977-78, The Flower Cart remained open during the summer months for the first time, with Helen deMarsh in charge of the program. The main activities were product labelling and wrapping for the bakery. There were a variety of recreational and social activities, including attendance at Kingswood Camp.

The Flower Cart was experiencing its own small industrial revolution as the program continued to grow and improve. Every day they demonstrated the abilities and needs of the "developmentally handicapped." New executive director Porter saw the value of staff training workshops and conferences to keep up on the latest research. Fittingly, the fall term began with a two-day in-service conducted by Carmela Enzinas on the subject of 'Goal Planning,' which focused on developing individualized programs for the trainees.

This approach was adopted and used in the so-called 'Upstairs' program, one of three distinct program streams, the others being the Carpentry Shop and The Baker's Dozen. The Upstairs program included apple picking and outdoor maintenance contracts and by the spring of 1978 extended to the re-webbing of lawn chairs. The nine participants were instructed by staff members Denise Aspinall, Don Deveau, and Helen deMarsh.

Director Joanne Porter enthusiastically hailed the marked change in approach and direction at The Flower Cart, including the fact that the trainees were totally involved in work programs and "there was never a need to resort to a fill-in activity." As a happy by-product of this contract work, she reported, "a decrease in behavioral problems," adding, "we notice a definite improvement in the trainees' attitude and self-esteem."

The jobs being carried out at The Flower Cart could hardly have been more eclectic. Over the winter, a contract was signed with Hostess Foods for the cutting, sorting, canceling, and bundling of potato chip bag coupons. The project generated almost $4,000 in revenue. The breadth of the contract exceeded expectations and the project was carried over to the next term. An arrangement was struck with Camera Corner for the production of picture frames. The Baker's Dozen increased their sales significantly as products were sold to 19 Annapolis Valley outlets and submarine sandwich buns were made for three area schools for a profit of almost $7,000.

The Carpentry Shop was extremely active as well. The picnic tables being produced proved very popular, with more than 80 tables ($3500 in revenue) sold to satisfied customers. Other lawn furniture was also repaired or constructed. In addition, the workers filled various special orders and helped with building maintenance, giving them exposure to plumbing, electrical work and further honing of their carpentry skills.

Brimming with optimism for the future, Porter looked forward to additional contracts and further developing the skill levels for the existing ones.

As the first decade drew to a close and the second one was about to begin, it was a time for contemplation and reflection. It had been a turbulent ten years for the young organization and an uncertain future lay ahead, a fact expressed in colourful terms by board chairman Hank Bosveld in the annual report for 1979-80: "From very humble beginnings and through the struggles of growing up, we can truthfully say now that perhaps we are getting into the stage of puberty and we know that it can go every which way." Bosveld was right of course. The future was full of both promise and pitfalls.

Nevertheless, there was a definite mood of optimism, tempered with a healthy dose of trepidation on the cusp of a new decade. The responsibility of shepherding The Flower Cart into the next stage was now in the hands of Joanne Porter, ironically a former neighbour of the DeWolfe family and first grade classmate of Linda DeWolfe. She become the first full-time Executive Director in 1977 and would remain as the keeper of the vision throughout most of the next decade.

The seventies are often referred to as the "me decade" but that was decidedly not the case at The Flower Cart where volunteerism and public service, generosity and the efforts of a selfless and dedicated staff helped keep The Flower Cart afloat. The first decade was in the books and the second was on the horizon.

CHAPTER FOUR: PROGRAM DIVERSITY

The Flower Cart continued to evolve to meet societal needs, even as the needs themselves have continued to evolve. Not surprisingly, this dynamic of change within change has often brought about something akin to an identity crisis within the organization. The continual state of flux within this micro environment mirrors changes in the wider community.

"As times changed, the provincial government moved toward de-institutionalization," recalls Joanne Porter. "Edmund Morris, who was the Minister of Community Services really appreciated what was going on at The Flower Cart and it became very collaborative."

It was sheer coincidence that as a child, Joanne Porter's storey-and-a-half brown house on Kent Avenue in Wolfville was situated directly across the street from the home of Jean and Owen DeWolfe. What impact this geographical fact played in her future career choices is uncertain, but the connection represents a direct and satisfying link to the roots of The Flower Cart organization. The Porters and DeWolfes were friends as well as neighbours, and Linda DeWolfe and Joanne Porter were playmates and briefly attended Wolfville Elementary together. She was blessed with the unique perspective of Jean, the visionary and Linda, the friend and future client. She knew first hand of Linda's predicament and she intimately understood the need for the creation of The Flower Cart.

Porter's 1977 appointment as executive director of The Flower Cart proved to be a game-changer. Her selection as the first full-time director in the workshop's 7-year history showed the board's satisfaction with the progress that had been made to date and reflected their confidence in an even more dynamic future. A milestone had been reached in the evolution of The Flower Cart.

Porter graduated from Acadia University in 1974 with a B.Sc. in Home Economics and in 1984 with her B.Ed., also from Acadia (after leaving The Flower Cart, she subsequently obtained her M.Ed.). Save for a few interruptions for travel, study, and childbirth - during which time Jim Oulton took over as interim director - she remained in the position until 1988, an eleven-year period of growth and change during which she oversaw the implementation of many innovative new programs designed to match the diversity of her clientele. The addition of new programs and the strengthening of others is just part of her enduring legacy.

Porter brought with her to the job a wealth of new ideas and a seemingly bottomless well of energy. She was determined to move forward, informed by the latest research from experts in the field of intellectual disabilities. "Originally The Flower Cart consisted of a director and two permissive license teachers," says Porter. "That was the term for those who didn't have B.Eds. The Department of Education later dissolved the permissive license concept and real teachers had to be found."

Looking back over her tenure, she is understandably proud of the progress that her team made in furthering the vision of the founders. Porter insists that by the time she assumed the reins, the infrastructure and staffing was well in place and she credits the hard work of her predecessors for that. "

"The Flower Cart exists because of Jean DeWolfe and Carmela Enzinas and Lorraine Boland. They were the movers and shakers in the conception and they did a really good job. Through Jean's daughter Linda, they identified why there was a need and what was needed, but things didn't happen overnight. They did their homework and consulted with a range of people across Canada. They conducted a few years of planning so that when they opened the doors to those four original women, they were ready to go. By the time I arrived in 1977, it was already running smoothly because so much of the foundation they created was solid.

"We were fortunate to have had a wonderful person in George Matthews at Community Services in Halifax. George was director of Community Services under Minister Edmund Morris. He absolutely believed in sheltered workshops and was a great supporter of what we were doing. George created a provincial council of sheltered workshops. I was on the council and you'd hear these horror stories from representatives of other workshops who were without any support.

"These Wolfville women had shown great foresight, great insight. They knew they wanted more than an arts and crafts experience for these young adults. There's nothing wrong with arts and crafts, but these were young women who they knew would be able to contribute to society, so they wanted more of a work base for them. They knew that from the outset.

"It has evolved, certainly, but it always had that work base as the key component, and I always felt so privileged when I was at those provincial meetings, because we weren't struggling like many other regions. We were in the forefront of what was happening in Nova Scotia."

NORMALIZATION

"The change agent, the abiding philosophy in the field of what's now called ID (Intellectual Disabilities) when I was there was deinstitutionalization," says Porter. "That was what was *au courant,* and Wolf Wolfensberger's research and writing about normalization was a big part of that. It was so strident, commanded everyone's attention and had such value in changing the way of thinking about the intellectually disabled. Policy makers' thinking changed incredibly, then practitioners' thinking changed, and their approaches changed.

Everyday people were altering their thinking because we were doing things differently. It was very strident.

"Before this research, we used to say, 'I don't know why the behaviour happens, I just want to change the behaviour.' Well, the fact is, you have to care why the behaviour happens because that's fundamental to changing it.

"Gentle teaching was introduced in the seventies and it replaced the institutional model that had been used. From the institutional mindset, if you were going to teach somebody to do a task, you were going to break it down into all its component parts and you were either going to teach them the first step and keep adding, or you were going to teach the last step and then the second to last step and the third. The idea of doing that, which is called backward chaining, is that you always finish with a finished product. The approach was kind of robotic and mechanical and it was about the task and not the person. Gentle teaching really didn't do anything differently except to have that established relationship with the person.

"At The Flower Cart, staff training didn't come until later. Our only training was having a good heart. Permissive license teachers didn't have to have formal training, they just had to have a special certificate. It could be anybody. Correction was a little bit prescribed, rather than learning how to adapt your response according to the person and the given situation.

"George (Matthews) believed that there were several Nova Scotia workshops like The Flower Cart – forerunners of what these places could and should be. Then there was another group that was striving in that direction, and a third group that was just stuck literally in church basements. Their values were fine, but he just thought that if we all came together we'd inspire each other and share. He even asked us to write the provincial standards and we developed a plan of what 'should' happen at these sheltered workshops. When he saw our plan, he said, 'I only have one comment, get rid of the word 'should' and put in 'will.'

"We were the only rural workshop and we were different because we had a public transport system, and it all came back to transportation. At that point, The Flower Cart only operated for nine months of the year because they were dependent on the school transportation service. My goal as director was to run a twelve-month program and we operated on grants for a couple of years.

"As Director, I was very hands-on, especially in the beginning. The part I liked most about The Flower Cart was the relationships with staff and participants. Of course, as it grew, the administrative part of my job grew too, but it was gratifying to watch the community's increasing acceptance of people with intellectual challenges. Nowadays, you see the concept working in schools as diversity is embraced. The Flower Cart has become part of the community.

"The bakery was already up and running when I got there. In fact, that was an original concept by the four founding women. Because I was now a 12-month employee, we tried to keep the bakery running for 12 months and that was hard. It required a shift in thinking. Participants had been used to having the summer off and now we had to arrange to get them there and of course there was no school board transportation support in the summer, so we had to work that out.

"Personnel was another huge issue. Initially professional bakers were sought out and hired but this approach proved less than ideal. If you're a professional baker, The Flower Cart is probably not your dream gig because you want other opportunities to use your entire skill set. If another opportunity comes along you take it, and that's what happened. We finally had to ask ourselves, 'What are we doing here?' In order to maintain continuity and bolster the training aspect of the bakery, it was decided to modify the hiring criteria.

"Despite the obstacles, the board never wavered in its commitment that the bakery should continue to play a major role in the overall program. I was determined that all workshop programs would become self-sustaining, including this one. In order to reach that goal, I had to move outside my comfort zone and into the world of business. What first attracted many of us to work at The Flower Cart was our community spirit but now there was a need for the Baker's Dozen to have a professional business model.

"We were a commercial bakery selling at commercial prices and yet we received government grants. There were some complaints about that. We had about a half million-dollar budget at that point, so I created flow charts and job descriptions that went far beyond what the social services and the community services called for. We even had to deal with labelling laws, an area that was foreign to all of us."

"During this time, the position of head baker changed hands several times. Pam O'Neil left in October, to be succeeded by Robert Grijm and then Paddy McMeeken and then Marlene Dodge arrived to replace assistant baker Faye Coolen. Thankfully, Marlene just stepped in to fill a void and it was then that things fell into place. When the staff became consistent, the product itself was more consistent.

The early growing pains experienced by the bakery were now a thing of the past and that the new business model was working. Executive Director Porter expressed confidence in The Baker's Dozen's ability to adapt and optimism for its long-term viability.

"Several years earlier, the focus of the bakery had been forced to change from production to training to accommodate the addition of new workers. The challenge had been to continue the training while producing sufficient baked good to maintain shelf space. These people were now trained in all aspects and capable of meeting higher production demands.

"In the late seventies there was a marked change in the direction of The Flower Cart. During this time, the trainees were totally involved in work programs and there was never a need to resort to a fill-in activity. Because of the contract work, there was a decrease in behavioral problems and we noticed a definite improvement in the trainees' attitude and self-esteem.

"From the beginning, the training was not academic. The Flower Cart was all about skills, labels, and attitudes. We wanted to make the participants contributing members of society to the best of their ability. In order to do that, the community had to be an integral part of their work experience. It was all in-house at the start, with the bakery serving as the centrepiece, followed by meal preparation, food preparation, and woodworking. We wanted to move toward more supported employment."

Part of Porter's strategy was to spread the word through service clubs.

"Suddenly The Flower Cart became a hot topic in the Valley. Service clubs like the Rotary Club would ask us in to speak. Our sales pitch, our mantra, became 'Invite us in and we'll be able to do the jobs that you want done, that you need done but don't want to do yourselves.' That included things such as making planting stakes, doing coupons, and picking apples and apple drops.

In 1979, when the move was on for community employment opportunities, one of our board members told us that a cleaning contract was coming up. We made a bid on it and secured a contract for cleaning the Municipal Building in Kentville. To have that as a transition was huge. We were so lucky with the board members and the staff members we had. They were so community-minded and were on other boards, so they had their hand on the pulse of the community.

The plan called for four full-time workers to be hired with one supervisory person overseeing the job. The initial contract was on a monthly basis. There was no ease-in period in the cleaning contract. We were the cleaners and we were expected to clean. Period. It was hard. It had been an open bid but we probably did get a break and got some points for who we were.

We held the contract for two years and it marked a major breakthrough for us. It offered high visibility. Picking apples was the only other time our clients had left the building to work. The community was just spectacular in their support.

We were thrilled with the contract because it followed a lot of planning and community education. It meant full time employment for people who had never worked before. We could leverage with other Valley businesses. At that time, 65% of the approved budget was generated from the Department of Social Services and 35% from strong community donations and bequeaths.

Those were in the good years, interest rates were 12% and we regularly just wrote a budget that said 10% over last year and they bought it and submitted it to the government. Service clubs continued to be an important source of financial support in the 80s with that remaining 35% coming from their contributions and from individual donors.

Attitudes had changed so much since I began in 1977. There was initial growth thanks to these initial contracts. The previous attitude was, 'Oh, isn't that nice. They have something to do.' They had a good heart, but a lot of people didn't see the potential, especially when we were strictly an in-house enterprise. I would say that by being isolated like that, we kept that false perception alive. But when we started to go out into the community a bit, things changed.

I think what it did was give the participants and the community insight into an undervalued group of people. And they could see the contribution that this group could make. Were they ever going to be the highest producers? No, but... for The Flower Cart participants, it gave them a sense of identity.

None of us are completely independent. We're all interdependent. I bring something and you bring something but together maybe we can accomplish even more. We do want to encourage the individual to grow and discover their strengths and support them in the areas that they're not strong in. Fostering individuality is a goal."

Paul Wehman's pioneering writing and research work served as the foundation for Porter's renewed emphasis on supported employment. Wehman, a Professor of Physical Medicine and Rehabilitation at Virginia Commonwealth University, was a noted authority in the field and his theories on transitioning from school to work and building business partnerships were the blueprints for change at The Flower Cart.

"While I was Director the trend in North America was toward supported employment," says Porter, "which was what it was called at the time. Paul Wehman, who is still writing, was our guide. We even began forays into Michelin, although not in a big way. We recognized that some Flower Cart participants who were working in the community needed support, and we tried to help them using this new model. We didn't do it very well, but we learned from it and could see that it was much better.

"Michelin was the first to accept us although at that time they said they were hesitant to have our folks as employees because they felt that our clientele was more at risk for injury. But it was them who said, 'You can have the space.' That was Michelin. We eased in that way and they were pretty impressed with what an untapped labor market our force was.

The research station also did that around the same time. We would send a group there with a staff member. They have all these plot stakes to indicate what the plant is, proper conditions for planting, and so on. Every year they had to be painted, and so we painted them. They could have brought them to us at The Flower Cart but they didn't and that was really neat. It opened up a whole new realm for our workers. All you need is a couple of converts like that - a couple of progressive organizations like the research station and Michelin – and then you can go to others and say, 'It works here and it works here.'

Kevin (West) used to go out into the community to try to find business opportunities. He thought it was important to actually get through the door where it's harder to say no. Once there, he could see the operation and say, 'We could do that for you.' Usually it was a job that the regular employees hated doing – not necessarily a menial job, but a task that was outside their production skills and job description.

We felt it was important that we maintain an employment atmosphere at The Flower Cart. Trainees and workers arrived at 8 am and left at 3 pm. That kind of structure helps develop skills and responsibility."

In 1981, the Wolfville Workshop and four other vocational services in the Valley combined forces to hire a marketing agent to market products and procure contracts. Jim Casey was hired as the marketing coordinator with additional responsibilities for public relations. Casey was responsible for direct selling of products from all centers including eleven wholesalers for items like Wolfville's peg boards, lawn furniture, child's furniture, planters, plaques and shields. The move brought quick results as all six workshops had reached 100% employment by the end of March 1982.

Around this time a picture framing department called Valley Framing was initiated. Under the guidance of staff member and future executive director Roger Tatlock, the program generated jobs such as frame assembly, refinishing, and the cutting of mattes. Tatlock oversaw the technical program and the training of four participants. Wholesale businesses contracted for about 600 frames and 200 mattes, grossing $7000.

In the early 80s, the contract that employed the largest number of people year-round was centered round a promotional campaign from Hostess Foods. It began with the counting and cancellation of coupons from the chip bags. In April 1981 alone, 51,500 coupons were processed for a dollar figure of $1,030.

Through the efforts of Jim Oulton and Jim Casey, the company was convinced to expand The Flower Cart's role. They were asked to assist the potato chip company in sorting, counting, and storage of the redeemed coupons on their return to the company. By the end of the fiscal year, trainees were processing four times the number of coupons compared to the start of the year, at only double the cost.

It was a win-win for The Flower Cart because it required a variety of tasks: pick-up, scanning for accuracy, sorting by coupon type, counting, packaging in bundles of one hundred, shelving by type, and invoicing, followed by return to the plant. The unique project provided employment for sixteen clients on a full or part time basis.

"We got the contract with Hostess Foods. Oh my god, that was huge," Oulton says. "The inside of the bags were stamped with a coupon so if you got a bag with a coupon in it you could take it back to the store and get a free bag of chips. They could write off the chips as a promotion, but their auditor said 'we need proof, you have to save each and every coupon.' So, we cut them out – one of those jobs no one wanted."

SCHOOL BOARD FINANCIAL CRISIS

From the time they first set up shop in the former New Minas Elementary School, The Flower Cart had enjoyed great moral and financial support from the Kings County District School Board, and that support continued well into Porter's time as director. In the early 1980s, the school board was contributing approximately $38,000 per year to The Flower Cart. The funds were used to pay instructor's salaries and carry out external maintenance at the site.

"Greg Ross, the Kings County superintendent, was always supportive," Joanne Porter recalls. "Students were permitted to take the school bus if they were on the regular bus route."

In 1984, The Flower Cart's very existence was threatened by a financial crisis as the Kings County District School Board was forced to discontinue its financial support. The move was prompted by a new special education clause in a recent funding formula for public education, set out by the NS Department of Education. The school system would henceforth be required to provide education for all students under 18 years of age, meaning that funding to The Flower Cart from the board could no longer be cost-shared with the Department of Education. The severed relationship ended the school board's significant yearly payment to The Flower Cart. Funds for teachers' salaries and upkeep of workshop facilities would have to be found elsewhere.

The legislation prompted outage and criticism from some concerned citizens. In a Letter to the Editor found in *The Kentville Advertiser* on July 11, 1984, Leo J. Deveau of Wolfville chided the board's decision to withdraw financial support. "The 'economic rationalization' process that the board has undertaken holds no human compassion or concern if it's to be done at the cost of the future livelihoods of the young adults working at The Flower Cart," wrote Deveau. Referring to the school system's "totem pole of priorities and self-interests," he referenced Patrick van Rensburg's observation that "A major function in schooling is role selection and selection always means rejection". He went on to say that, "The Flower Cart in essence should be a role model for the whole educational process that the school board oversees. Namely tying together the educational and practical applications of learning. The consciousness of The Flower Cart participants develops within a whole social process of experience and activity, of learning and collective work. The Flower Cart is a business and a classroom. Just think what we could do if all classrooms in the county could be like that!"

While the Department of Social Services would continue to pay the majority of the operating costs, the remainder would have to come from work contracts carried out by trainees coupled with financial support from the community. The withdrawal meant that a revised budget had to be created and sent to the Department of Social Services to make up for the shortfall. Board chairman Hank Bosveld indicated that a direct appeal to the public for assistance might be required in order to maintain the operations. The change also meant that The Flower Cart could now only admit adults with intellectual disabilities that were 21 years of age or older, rather than the usual cut off age of 18.

"The board is now at a critical stage and in the next while some important long-term decisions will have to be made," cautioned acting director Jim Oulton. Fortunately, the joint marketing of

Flower Cart services under Porter and Oulton had succeeded in securing 43 contract jobs for Flower Cart participants.

Porter has a more pragmatic and forgiving view of the split and is adamant that the altered relationship with the school board was amicable, and that the board did their best to avoid disruption. "Even after school board funding was ended by the provincial government, the school board continued to work with us every step of the way. During that transition, we had Department of Education people meeting with us to see how they could avoid leaving us in the lurch. The Kings County School Board did their best to work with our board."

"We obtained ownership of the building which was something wonderful. The municipality declared it surplus to their needs so that we could buy it. I want to make it really clear that the school board didn't drop us. They were terrific, and we sat with the department people in Halifax and tried to work it out. In the end it came down to us not meeting their criteria for accreditation, but they tried."

To help mitigate the loss of revenue from the Department of Education, one cost saving option that was suggested was to combine the Flower Cart and the Wolfville Group Home, where Kevin West was director.

"We received calls from parents saying they'd pay for their child to come from 18-21. The school board didn't argue. They knew that what we were doing was best for a certain group of kids. We called it work experience so they would get by the graduation year rule. Brett Woodbury at the Department of Education was trying his best to help."

END OF AN ERA

One of Porter's most noteworthy accomplishments was the development of the school-to-work model and she was ideally qualified to do it. "She was the driving force," says Kevin West. "I liked

Joanne because she wasn't intimidated by anyone or anything. She spoke her mind and was no wallflower. She could be blunt at times. She was a true leader and always stepped up, even at the provincial level. She was extremely smart and very collaborative and could stand up and speak persuasively."

Of the school-to-work program, West says "we were one of the first workshops to do that, mostly due to Joanne Porter. Joanne set up that model and then went to work at the school system and helped to initiate it. She pitched the ball and caught it too."

The program was extremely successful. Designed for students in the last four years of high school, it became part of the school curriculum at Horton High, West Kings High, and Central Kings for students to come to the sheltered workshop to work. They came for a morning, an afternoon, or a full day up to five days a week with a per diem being charged to the school board after three days.

"The school buses would pick up our people and take them to Horton and then a bus would take them here," says West. "King's Transit was also excellent. One time one of our participants had a seizure and the driver made a detour to his home.

"There was an arrangement with the school board which was responsible for those kids that allowed them to come to The Flower Cart. They gave us this building and heated and maintained it. They gave us the equivalent of one teaching salary which allowed us to get two workers/instructors."

During her tenure as Executive Director, Porter took time off to travel and to earn her B.Ed. from Acadia. Her experience as director had prepared her well. "The Flower Cart trained me better than any program," she maintains. "When I later left for the regular school system in 1988, I was able to use the skills I developed at The Flower Cart to run resource programs at Kings County Academy."

Despite the loss of one of their most dynamic and effective directors, Porter's connection to The Flower Cart would continue to pay benefits long after her departure.

"She inherited a rundown building and through her leadership she made us a viable enterprise," says West. "She oversaw the expansion of the building into what we have today."

She was responsible for transforming the bakery from just a training program to a viable, soon-to-be thriving business. Under her watch, strides were made in obtaining contract work and piece work for Hostess and other businesses such as the framing shop for The Camera Corner.

In early 1986, following five years of planning and fundraising, The Flower Cart announced plans for a much-needed renovation and expansion. Between the steadily growing clientele and the expanded course and program offerings, the existing space was no longer adequate. The estimated cost of the expansion was placed at $375,000 and a large bequest enabled construction to commence. Linda DeWolfe, representing The Flower Cart workers, and chairman of the board of directors, Hank Bosveld, turned the first sod to signal the official start although additional funding would still be needed to offset operating costs, capital, and related expenses.

Executive Director Porter was quick to point out that the infrastructure improvements would also help to facilitate more interaction with the community and allow the door at the sheltered workshop "to swing both ways." One way of doing this was to add a café and a bakery outlet that would be open to the public. A catering component was also planned, as was the direct marketing of carpentry products.

Meanwhile, the Wolfville Workshop had been established to support the eight people living in their group home. "The Department of Social Services got the idea that we should combine with Wolfville," recalls Porter. "This happened in the middle of us doing major renovations and so they saw an opportunity to build these guys in. We were full, didn't have staffing, didn't have whatever so they started their own workshop, which Kevin West operated. It was wonderful and had something we couldn't offer - a 1:5 staff member-student ratio.

"The Wolfville group remained in that location and our board took over the running of it so for a while there were two different Flower Cart locations," says Porter. In 1986, a bequest from Jean Gibson made possible major renovations of the Flower Cart building. With the completion of building expansion at 9412 Commercial St. facility, the Workshop location in Wolfville closed its doors for good and the staff and participants moved to New Minas as part of the newly formed Developmental Services division.

"The decision was finally made to combine the two into one building. The Wolfville group moved their operation to our facility in New Minas. The two now had the same board of directors. Kevin was Manager and I was Director. Kevin was amazing. He really had an ability to think outside the box."

Trainees at the carpentry shop were busy making bird houses and feeders as well as creating what would become very popular: picnic tables. They worked with nearby Mermaid Theatre to design and construct puppet boxes, after which the Upstairs group would assemble the puppets for the boxes.

Another progressive innovation was introduced in 1986 and reflected both the impact of the sheltered workshop and the changing attitudes of society. A workers' council was formed. Porter told a reporter for *The Kentville Advertiser* that she had evolved as a director and learned to be receptive to ideas that came from the intellectually disabled participant. "Mental retardation doesn't mean a person has to be protected," said Porter. "It means that the teaching of anything has to be more intensive."

WORKERS' COUNCIL

The workers' council was a major initiative that would continue to evolve under future directors, including Porter's successor Jim Oulton who, as a staff member, was involved from the outset. Porter recalls the genesis of the concept.

"My thinking had evolved during my time as director and I had learned to be receptive to ideas that came from the intellectually disabled participants.

"The idea of a workers' council came out of the provincial council that all the sheltered workshop directors belonged to. George Matthews from the Department of Community Services started that council and then we were expected to have our own regional councils as well. For example, the directors of Kings County workshops included me, Bernie Jackson in Aylesford, and the director of the Wolfville Group Home before we combined. It actually included the whole Valley because there was the Revolving Door in Lawrencetown and Conway in Digby and the Windsor Workshop. The Rehab Centre in Waterville also had a workshop that was funded through the rehab called The Plank and Hammer, and their director was included in our regional group."

"When the directors met, it was The Flower Cart that said that participants who actually work in the workshops need a similar avenue to express themselves and be heard. I was representing our whole organization, but I needed to represent it knowing what the staff's issues were, but I also had to represent the participants' issues.

"The People First movement was a workers' council and ours was formed by the participants. It gave them a voice, but it came with responsibilities too. This was at the time of worker's rights, yes, but workers responsibilities were attached to those rights.

"It started out mostly as a social thing. 'Let's have a party!' Well that's great, but all of a sudden a group of people who had always had things done for them were being asked to make decisions. They were deciding the type of music they wanted and not realizing that yes, it was great to organize a party, but you had to find out if it was okay to have the party at The Flower Cart, and how do you get the key, and who do you want to be there, and what staff people should be there, and who are you going to invite, and so on. Eventually it became a chance to address more significant issues.

"When the renovation to the building was being done, the workers' council decided on paint colours in their various areas – not my office, I got to pick that. They got to decide theirs and I got to decide mine.

"They met weekly, staff directed at first, but that wasn't the intent. It soon became staff supported, and that's really what it was. That was needed just to bring some structure. What are you going to do at your meeting? That's the support they were being given at work and in their lives."

Roger Tatlock recalls how the idea of the workers' council originated and quickly caught on. "When I worked with Jim Oulton as a front-line staff member, he was always the first to champion the workers. He was always saying, 'Let's listen to them. Let's poll them. Let's ask them questions.' When Jim became executive director, the workers' council idea took sharper form. It was all about participants working together because Jim was really, really big on being on the side of the clients and listening to them and enabling their voices to be heard.

"I saw it as worthy endeavour for participants. I told them 'You don't have a voice with the executive director on a regular basis so I'm going to stand in front of you as a group at least once a month and hear what you have to say. If you want to throw a brick at me, throw a brick – and I have some things to say to you too!' So we kept minutes and we had agendas and it was like a regular staff meeting.

"Today I'm sure they're at an even more autonomous level because at that time it was 'We are the employer, we're the leader' and I took it as a personal commitment: I will stand in front of you every month and hear what you have to say.

"You had to follow an agenda, my agenda. It was my meeting and you had to be recognized, you had to speak to the floor. It was a process, a learning process for me and for them but that's the format that I created. Now I hope that it has evolved to the point where it's more self-governed. If so, it's a good evolution."

THE WORK IS THE THING

"The founders absolutely thought The Flower Cart should be work oriented, a sheltered workshop. There's no question about that. That's why it had such a strong foundation. I didn't have to convince anybody because they saw the purpose. They saw the underlying value. The Flower Cart was just so fortunate to be blessed with the foresight of these women," says Porter.

"Later, when Roger Tatlock came on as executive director they didn't enjoy the level or ease of funding that I did. He did have to raise some of that money because donations alone wouldn't be enough. So, he had to install even more of a business model and still hold onto the reason we're here. It was just another stage in our evolution.

During my time as director, I never did have to deal with the retirement of participants, but retirement became an issue later on. If you can't complete a full work life it's the community that's going to provide for you. It might be recreation and exercise oriented; it might be volunteering with the SPCA. I believe that leisure is a huge part of life, and retirement. During my own working life, my whole identity was through my work and my volunteer work revolved around what my kids were involved in. Now my kids have moved on and I've retired, and I've had to look at what's out there differently.

The same is true of Flower Cart participants. That community is no different. I think there really are those three big aspects to a person's life: it's a work life, a residential life, and then there is a leisure time, getting together with friends or enjoying an organization or volunteering differently."

MAINTAINING THE MOMENTUM

When Joanne Porter left The Flower Cart for a position in the Kings County school system in 1988, long-time front-line staff worker Jim Oulton took over as executive director. He continued in the position through 1992, a productive span that saw Oulton continue the work started under Porter and initiate many of his own.

Oulton had served as interim director a few times when Porter was on leave. The first time was between September 1983 and May 1984 when Porter left to earn her education degree from Acadia University. It was during this time that Department of Education policy forced the Kings County school board to end their financial support, resulting in a funding crisis for the organization.

But not all the news from 1984 was bad. The Flower Cart was bustling, working diligently to develop programs to satisfy their ever-growing population. "People have individual needs," said Oulton. "The more diversity we have to offer, the more we can meet those needs at our shops."

The Baker's Dozen bakery was now thriving, producing several thousand loaves of bread, as well as rolls and cookies every month. Other activities going on behind those doors included a picture framing operation, a meals-on-wheels program and, at any given time, several carpentry projects, including the refinishing of desks for the school board.

In an early April speech at the Wolfville Rotary Club, acting director Jim Oulton explained the numerous contract jobs that the 43 trainees had worked on in recent months. The firms involved included Scotian Gold, Agriculture Canada, and General Foods. The contracts were the result of efforts by Marion Watson, a marketing specialist working on behalf of five sheltered workshops in the Valley. This contract procurement officer was familiar with the range of abilities of workshop trainees and the needs of the business community, making her well-positioned to submit tenders and negotiate contracts based on the ability to deliver. Said Oulton, "When she makes a tender, it's strictly in business terms and there's no sentiment involved."

In November 1985 five staff members from The Flower Cart attended training sessions given by Wolf Wolfensberger on the subject of Social Role Valorization (SRV). Two years earlier, in 1983,

Wolfensberger had introduced the term to replace and update the principle of normalization that he had introduced in his 1972 book *The Principle of Normalization in Human Services*. SRV is a powerful set of concepts that can be used to make positive change for individuals disadvantaged because of their social status.

The basic theory is that society tends to identify groups of people as different and of less value than everyone else, and in response it lays the groundwork for addressing and mitigating the effect of such devaluing. The principle of Social Role Valorization would become a guiding principle for The Flower Cart and other organizations for adults with intellectual disabilities.

Oulton also filled in for Joanne during her maternity leave in 1987. His familiarity with the position and knowledge of programs and systems made for a seamless transition, and allowed the organization to maintain the momentum that had built under his predecessor. "Our objective now is to develop and expand community-based employment opportunities with adults living with a mental handicap," he wrote in his first annual report in March of 1989.

He was especially keen to promote and facilitate self-advocacy for Flower Cart participants. Speaking directly to them, he openly called for greater involvement. "I encourage you, the adult participants in The Flower Cart employment options, to speak out in your own interest," he said at the time. "You and the significant people in your life must continue to challenge us to be better and more effective at assisting you to meet your own needs."

Oulton was also committed to keeping the programs relevant to a very diverse clientele. "We continue to develop programs that would be useful to a wide range of clients. People have individual needs," he said. "The more diversity we have to offer, the more we can meet those needs at our shops."

"I'd speak to service clubs and tell them that it was lovely to get donations and that we couldn't get by without them, but we also need work contracts. I'd say, we need paying jobs and we have something to offer. We can provide solutions to you. That was a new concept. And we'd use those community connections. The head of Hostess, for example, was a member of the Kentville Rotary Club.

Jean DeWolfe *(top left)* was a founding member of The Flower Cart. Her daughter Linda *(right)* with board chair Hank Bosveld, turned the first sod to signal the start of an expansion in the 1980s.

Lisa Hammett Vaughan (right) presents Shawn Biggs with the First Annual Biggs Award. Each year it is awarded to an exceptional participant.

A photo of original The Flower Cart building prior to the expansion project. Note the actual flower cart in the bottom right, said to be the namesake for the organization.

An updated rendering of the proposed new facility that will be located at 9503 Commercial Street in New Minas. The 23,100 sq. ft. facility will mean increased production opportunities and a projected 22% increase in client service capacity.

Of particular note, everything will be on one floor and much more accessible, and nearly all enterprises will operate and collaborate under one roof. There will also be an outdoor work area and the location, adjacent to the Louis Millet Community Complex, opens possibilities for access to recreation and leisure programs never before possible.

Above: The Flower Cart's Dawna Havill *(far left)* and Gay Clarke *(left)* were on hand to greet former Prime Minister Stephen Harper when he visited the Michelin Waterville plant. Below: Roger Tatlock *(left)* welcomes Carrie Hemmings, The Flower Cart's first Financial Director.

Above: Bonnie Wright proudly displays the beloved
Baker's Choice Fine Foods fresh bread.

Below: Devin MacLeod assembled a washer toss
game for the Wood Working program.

Above: Doug Butler works on packaging for Made with Local Real Food Bars. Below: Brian Greencorn *(left)* disassembles scrap computers for recycling. Tracy Sheffield *(right)* has worked in several departments for The Flower Cart, and says she likes the bakery best.

Top: Leah Phinney organizing the inventory at Consignor's Place in New Minas.

Left: Every Wood Working item is stamped with The Flower Cart logo.

Right: Jeff Kelly became the Executive Director in 2014 and has navigated the organization through some incredible challenges ever since.

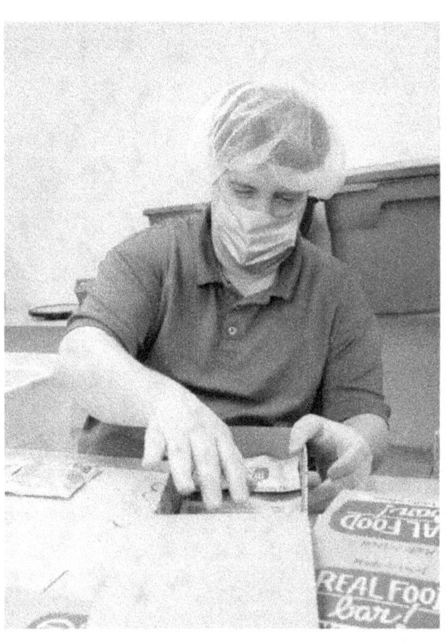

Above: A sign of the times. On the left, Evan Hiltz poses for a photo that was used in an early 1990's advertisement. Years later Evan is still working at The Flower Cart, and he shows off his trendy face mask that was required wearing for much of 2020. Below: Marlene Coleman *(left)* helps Made with Local founder Sheena Russell make her patented Real Food Bars in the What's Cooking? Commercial Kitchen.

Above: The Flower Cart Group's Building Opportunities Campaign Lead gift contributor Gus Smith *(left)* from Nova Industrial, with Devin MacLeod, December 2019.

Below: Valley Credit Union's CEO and President Len Eles and Board Chair Martin Gillis also made a substantial donation as The Flower Cart wrapped up a successful campaign for the new facility.

CHAPTER FIVE: WORK WITH PURPOSE

"Any strategy to reduce inter-generational poverty has to be centred on work, not welfare. Not only because work provides independence and income, but because work provides order, structure, dignity, and opportunities for growth in people's lives."

-Former US President Barack Obama in *The Audacity of Hope: Thoughts on Reclaiming the American Dream* (2006)

ROGER TATLOCK: A PROFILE

With the passing of the Porter-Oulton era, The Flower Cart management board searched for a new administrator to consolidate the advances that had been made to date and take the organization to the next level. That person would have big shoes to fill, but they didn't have to look far.

Roger Tatlock, a native of Glace Bay, Cape Breton, was sought out by Oulton and hired as Executive Director of The Flower Cart in 1992.

"Joanne Porter had taken us from a single workshop to be part of a provincial organization. She had become a leader within that organization. Roger took that baton and brought it forward in terms of clearer staff policies and procedures, accountability and benefits," says Kevin West.

Tatlock was entering the final year of a B.Sc. program at Acadia University when his department head took him aside and informed him that a new course was about to be introduced focused on "mental retardation." The goal was to develop leaders for the industry in Nova Scotia. "He said I might be good at it, so I made the decision to do just that," recalls Tatlock, who subsequently graduated with a B.Sc. in Psychology with Specialization in Mental Retardation. His decision would prove to be life-altering, not just for himself but for those whose lives would be enriched by his lifelong commitment to the intellectually disabled.

It was on Cape Breton Island, in the hardscrabble landscape of the coal mines and coke ovens, that his social conscience was forged and his world view shaped. The mining culture was built on workers' rights and the belief in the inherent dignity of work. For Tatlock, these concepts and the battles to attain them were grounded in reality, not theory, and they set the course for his future.

The new Acadia University program would set the course of Tatlock's life. "I spent my entire working life in that field and retired in that field," he points out. "The people that started that program were right. There needed to be leadership development. It gave me a foundation that was professional because at the time, other than institutions, there was no professionalization of our industry in Nova Scotia. They set that standard."

"I first started working at The Flower Cart in 1980, three months before I graduated from Acadia," he says. The new job also represented a return to his roots, deepening his commitment to the undervalued people in society. "I worked full time as a front-line staff person as one of Joanne Porter's employees for four years."

West remembers Tatlock as a force of raw energy that swept into New Minas like a crusader. Initially he was unsure of what to make of the passionate young man. "When I first knew Roger, I wasn't impressed," he admits. "In fact, he was a pain in the ass. He was all about Cape Breton coal miners and unions. He was all for unions and advocacy for staff and workers' rights."

The Flower Cart proved to be a wonderful training ground for a young man with a social conscience and an endless supply of energy. While working under director Joanne Porter, Valley Framing was his major job. This experience, which included elements of business collaboration and vocational teaching, was a perfect preparation for what would become his life work.

"They did custom jobs," recalls West. "Camera Corner was our primary customer and supplied the material. We had a mitre saw, framing, and mat cutters."

After four years, Roger and his wife Kim, a staffer that he had met at The Flower Cart, were eager for a change and a chance to grow in his chosen field. The province of New Brunswick beckoned. "I left the Flower Cart to go to New Brunswick because they had started to de-institutionalize the two major mental health facilities in the province in Campellton and Saint John. They wanted to enable intellectually disabled people to live in the community and they were throwing a lot of money at the initiative. The Canadian Association for the Mentally Retarded in Fredericton was well financed, and they were pushing hard for the province to de-institutionalize.

"We decided to move to Moncton. My wife was from there and was familiar with the area. There was no shortage of good jobs, jobs that were on the cutting edge promoting a progressive agenda, trying to do the right thing.

I worked there for 9 years, taking a year and a half off to teach at the community college. We brought people out of Centra-Care (the century old structure had originally known as the New Brunswick Lunatic Asylum, then the Provincial Hospital for Nervous Diseases, and the Provincial Hospital prior to 1978) who had been born in that institution. I was happy to be in New Brunswick because of the stuff they were doing, the support they were giving staff, and the training. My mantra was, 'You're not baking bread, you're changing society.'"

It was in New Brunswick that Tatlock encountered the single biggest change agent in his professional life. His name was Wolf

Wolfensberg and he was already legendary and one of the most respected voices in the field of intellectual disabilities. The New Brunswick Department of Community Services had brought him to the province from his base at Syracuse University to help carry out their de-institutionalization agenda.

"The oracle for me in my career was Wolf Wolfensberg and his ground-breaking work in the area of social role valorization," says Tatlock. "I worked directly with Wolf doing assessments at facilities in New Brunswick and was his disciple at the time."

Tatlock was also responsible for ushering in a high professional standard in what is now a human services core competency. "They brought Non-Violent Crisis Intervention into the province and mandated that every service provider that worked with people coming out of the institutions would be trained in it. I went to Milwaukee, Wisconsin to receive advanced training in their techniques, so the people of New Brunswick invested a lot of time and money in me to help me develop."

Tatlock was well positioned to see the big picture and understand the healing properties of purposeful work. "Why are people doing what they're doing? I firmly believe that most people who work don't know why they're working. They work for a paycheque but fail to see the bigger picture. What we tried to do in New Brunswick was to get people to adopt a new paradigm, and not to say that intellectually disabled people are sick or that they're mentally ill, or not that they're perpetual children. At that time, they were seen as people who were devalued."

Tatlock was in the right place at the right time, at the forefront of a movement that was bold and transformational. It necessitated a radical change of thinking and approach, and encompassed governments, support agencies, and the public. It was a daunting task.

"To their credit, the New Brunswick government saw their job was to move the people from institutions. The prevailing thought had been, 'You're so devalued that we're going to keep you in a big house on the hill.' Now it was to be 'Oh, you can live in my neighborhood and we can work shoulder-to-shoulder in business and industry.'

So, to take that mindset where a whole culture was brought up with pity for these poor people, to move from that type of historic thinking around that population to, 'We just haven't embraced them into our community like other devalued groups.

Being a Cape Bretoner and coming out of families that supported unions and coal miners that were devalued... yeah, I was brought up in that environment of achieving a valued status, being valued as a worker, being valued as a citizen. That really spoke to me. It made me pound the desk, you know? I'd be at meetings sitting at desks with workers saying 'Come on, you have to stop thinking like this.' I did it because it was important to change the mindset."

RETURN TO THE FLOWER CART

It was at that point that a former colleague from Nova Scotia came calling. "One day Jim Oulton was in Moncton looking at vocational services in the city and invited me out to supper. Jim was leaving The Flower Cart as executive director and told me that I should consider applying for the job."

Tatlock found the idea intriguing and after due consideration he and Kim decided to accept the challenge. He applied for the position and was hired, returning to his former workplace in the Valley as executive director of The Flower Cart, armed with vast experience in the field, a deep philosophical foundation, and a burning desire to use these assets to drive change in his home province.

When Tatlock returned to The Flower Cart, this time as director, Kevin West, saw a big change in the former employee. "The fire was still there but it was redirected," says West. "He had matured a lot and learned a lot. Roger had very high standards. He brought so many ideas with him. He wanted to upgrade the staff and upgrade the service we provided. Right off the bat he instituted a higher level of professionalism. He was concerned about how we deliver our service and how we conduct ourselves as a staff.

"He had taught at the community college in Moncton and had run a residential program. He was steeped in the philosophy of Wolfensberger on SRV. It was a change for us. Before that, with Jo-anne Porter, we had followed a gentle teaching model, but the thinking had evolved."

"Roger was a good teacher. He taught us Non-Violent Crisis Intervention and he made it fun, using a very hands-on and practical model. It was not dry or boring, it was relevant to our experience. Even today people recall those sessions. He took us to the next level."

"It wasn't warm and fuzzy, but it was good, it was solid," said West. "People appreciated the fact that if he was wrong he'd say so."

It wasn't long before Tatlock soon discovered that the province of Nova Scotia hadn't progressed as rapidly in their thinking when compared with their neighbouring province.

"When I came back, the political will wasn't yet there in Nova Scotia like it was in NB," he says. In fact, parts of Nova Scotia still clung to the outdated model of institutionalization, not in the physical buildings sense perhaps, but in the culture, in their attitudes toward the intellectually disabled. At that time, Nova Scotia had one of the highest per capita percentages of institutionalized people of any jurisdiction anywhere in the world. That thinking doesn't change overnight. It was scary.

Those institutions were for all kinds of people. I just refer to them all as 'the Big House.' What label you want to use for the Big House, whether it's jail or psychiatric facility... doesn't matter. The physical changes were happening, but the institutional mindset was slower to change. Intellectually disabled people were still isolated and set apart from regular society.

The goal was to move them to a farm far out in the country, put a fence around it and let them all live there. It sounds like science fiction in this day and age, but it was a reality. Many inmates were born, lived their entire lives, and died in those places. And many had no reason to be there at all.

It's the age-old question. Is the government in a position of leadership or is it in the position of responding to the citizens and the voters? There was obviously a critical mass in New Brunswick that pushed the political will in a progressive direction. Would that have happened in Nova Scotia? Well, I think it did happen eventually.

We can all have our own thoughts but when I look back, it's obvious that these people were devalued. The valued people weren't put into poor farms. So, what is the test of a society? How they treat their most vulnerable people. I think you must try to move the most vulnerable from 'the other' to 'us,' from the devalued to the valued.

Whenever I talk to students or laypeople I always say, 'Ok, who's been devalued as a group in the past in Nova Scotia?' Hands immediately go up. 'Women were definitely devalued.' 'Black people were devalued.' 'First Nations people were devalued.' 'Homosexuals were devalued. These groups have all done a really good job of changing that in the last generation. It's amazing how they've all gone from a devalued to a valued status."

Today Tatlock speaks in the same evangelical tones he once used when challenging and motivating his staff. "So, my follow-up question is always: well, who is the next group? Who's the next population to move from a devalued status to a valued status?"

As for The Flower Cart itself, Tatlock found it "enlightened in the 'concept' but not in the methodology. The progress at The Flower Cart was evolutionary, not revolutionary. And when you look around now, The Flower Cart to me is like an iceberg. You see the building in New Minas and that's just the tip of the iceberg. The work is behind the scenes, the part of the iceberg hidden under the water, where clients go to work, pay their bills, are good to their husbands and wives, and raise their children. That's the work."

TEARING DOWN THE BIG HOUSE MENTALITY

Although he has since been steeped in research that didn't exist when The Flower cart, began, Tatlock continued to be impressed by the foresight of the founders and the continued relevance of the original vision.

"I refer back to a document that was written in 1974. They wrote right that this document was a blueprint for the future. This is what we seek. I used to read it when I was executive director. Every once in a while, I'd be sitting at my desk and think, 'Oh god, what are we doing here?' Or I'd run into Mrs. DeWolfe or I'd actually call her just to get a grounding. 'What are we doing here again?' and that document that they wrote – it will stand the test of time.

If you read the words about helping people take responsibility, helping people get a place in the community, it's affirming. I like the fact – and I was often criticized when I worked there – that they wrote in that document, that work is paramount."

THE MICHELIN BREAKTHROUGH

When Michelin Tire opened the first of their three tire plants in Nova Scotia in 1971, the province had good reason to celebrate. Michelin is the second largest tire manufacturer in the world, producing approximately 190,000 tires a year, a 14% market share. In addition to a long list of other products and services, including the renowned Michelin Guide, they design and make tires for airplanes, cars, bikes, heavy equipment, heavy-duty trucks, motorcycles, and even the space shuttle. The 130-year old French corporate giant has a presence on every continent and in 17 countries and employs more than 114,000 people worldwide. Their global footprint, or tire print to be precise, includes 69 manufacturing facilities.

The Granton, Pictou County facility began making tires in 1971 and the Bridgewater plant followed shortly after. The Waterville Michelin plant opened in 1982 and was focused on the production of tires for the heavy-machinery market.

There's a curious symmetry in the fact that Michelin opened its first Nova Scotia plant just a year after The Flower Cart came into existence although at that time, any connection between the two very different enterprises would have been difficult to foresee. In the intervening years, Michelin has grown to become the largest manufacturing employer in Nova Scotia and the second largest exporter of goods. The economic benefits from Michelin are felt throughout the province with 3500 direct jobs and untold numbers of indirect employment created to support them.

Like Michelin, the Flower Cart has also grown steadily since 1970. What was once a small sheltered workshop for intellectually disabled adults has spread its wings and their trainees are employed in a variety of jobs throughout the Kings County business community. The common denominator between the two is the work.

Michelin needs specialized workers that they can rely on to meet the high standards of quality that they demand. The Flower Cart is uniquely qualified to train and supervise these workers. Both organizations have a long-term commitment to the Valley and a highly compatible vision for the future. As a progressive organization, Michelin realizes that diversity and inclusion are ultimately good for business.

"We care about creating a purpose-driven culture where employees feel empowered by their individual contributions," says David Stafford, Chief Human Resources Officer for Michelin North America. At the Waterville plant these are more than just noble words. You can witness inclusiveness in action every day as dozens of Flower Cart clients go to work and experience the satisfaction of working with colleagues toward a common goal. Work with purpose, indeed.

There were many defining moments during Tatlock's time as director, but none bigger, symbolically, inspirationally, or in practical terms than the deal that was struck with tire giant Michelin. It was the culmination of Tatlock's commitment to the concept of dignity through work and represented the goal of The Flower Cart founders writ large. The dove-tailing of The Flower Cart's goals and Michelin's needs is one of the greatest chapters in the 50-year history of the organization. But it didn't happen by accident.

The groundwork for the Michelin deal was done years before the actual contract was signed. It took place at a board meeting early in his time as director and without it, the nature of The Flower Cart might be a very different today. Roger Tatlock was about to make one of the most important and risk-laden moves in his tenure. Everything he envisioned hinged on the result.

"The achievements that I'm most proud of all hearken directly back to the founding document. People wanting to work. People contributing to the industry and the community in which they live. So, the social enterprise aspect was really important to me, crucially important."

Tatlock opted to throw down the gauntlet, challenging the board members to honour the words recorded in the report from the very first annual general meeting. In doing so he quoted a passage from the report.

"The goal of The Flower Cart Sheltered Workshop is basically that of helping each young person develop and function to the full extent of his or her abilities. To achieve this goal, we have tried to offer a program of involving methods of exposure, training, and experience to help them cope more adequately with the various requirements of production, the family, and the community."

Conventional sources of money, such as service clubs and government organizations had been the traditional revenue stream supplemented by whatever monies Flower Cart participants raised from their various activities and sales. Tatlock needed the support of the board in pursuing new revenue streams.

The Flower Cart was in need of additional financial resources and Tatlock decided that it was time to tackle the issue head on. The outcome would have long term repercussions well beyond the immediate need, but the financial challenge also offered him an opportunity to set the course for the future.

Tatlock needed the support of the board in pursuing new revenue streams. "It was also a risk," he admits. "I remember that first board meeting. I was standing in front of the board saying we need some money. Now I had the slides, and I told them I could put a slide deck together and go around to service clubs and other groups with my hand out and do all of that because there's lots of good things to say about The Flower Cart as a worthy place to donate. Or we could make money! I think we need to make money. "

Having stated his case, Tatlock nervously awaited the board's reaction, knowing how much was riding on the response. "I remember that so clearly and that was 25 or more years ago. I was taking a risk. If that board had maintained that we're a charity and we live and die on the benevolence of our community, I would have been out bumming money. I opened my mouth because I believed in the founding vision of people in the community working shoulder to shoulder with intellectually handicapped people and contributing to their industry."

"That's your contribution and you should be proud of that, you contributed to your community. The social enterprise concept was extremely important to me, but it was a risk," says Tatlock.

When the answer finally came he breathed a sigh of relief. "Luckily, the board said yes, we're going to make some money."

With the board onside, the next step was to turn theory into practice. Tatlock had to come up with a plan of action. The dog had finally caught his tail. Now what?

"I thought, how do we do that? Because I'm certainly not a businessman, but I remember clearly saying, 'We have to get some employers to hire our people. We need to do it in some way shape or form. Like on a contract or something like that. Who are we going to go after? And I want to go after them and have them look us in the eye and say F-off!'

We're going to go after them. And I used that language. If they don't tell you to F-off, arrange another appointment and go back. Initially, we targeted a major employer but they were unionized and said no, it couldn't happen. So, we said, what's the largest non-unionized environment in the Valley? Michelin. Let's go and get Michelin and let's keep going until they tell us to F-off. And they never did."

In 2006, Gay Clarke became the first full-time Michelin Contract Coordinator for The Flower Cart. She remained in the position until health issues forced her to retire in 2013. During her tenure, the relationship between the tire giant and the supported workshop blossomed.

"When I started in 2006," Clarke recalls, "we had six employees at Michelin. When I had to leave in 2013 after I was injured in a car accident, I had 53. Michelin did everything they could to accommodate me. I had a special pass, so I could park around the building right next to my office. I tried everything to stay but I just couldn't do it."

Clarke was known for her ability to grow the contract, but also for her passionate advocacy for her contract workers. She had no qualms about going into meetings, raising her voice and slamming doors if it meant her team was going to be treated fairly.

"More than anything Gay taught me that this job follows you home every day," says Matt Clairmont, who became the Contract Coordinator in 2014. "Compassion and commitment to your participants stays with you, and when the phone rings and it's one of our contract workers in need, there is no such thing as off-hours."

PARTNERS IN EMPLOYMENT

In 1993, shortly after Roger Tatlock became executive director, The Flower Cart took over sponsorship of the Partners in Employment (PIE), a project that works directly with employers to create competitive employment opportunities for Flower Cart clients.

The PIE program had been highly successful in partnering workers with employers for interviews, training, work visits, and ultimately, employment. Where once it was based on direct client intakes, it came to include referrals from other community agencies as the focus shifted to supported employment.

Among the services available to work candidates were employment counseling, career exploration, and decision making. The program also offered referrals to training and other community services, job search support, placement, and on-the-job orientation, training, and support. PIE was also responsible for the Transition-to-Work (TTW) project, initiated to service individuals entering the workforce.

Leah Reagh, a TTW participant in 2009, spoke of her own experience. "TTW is a place that doesn't judge people, no matter what," she said. "They look at you and they see you, they let you in with a smile and a big thumbs up, and they let you grow and change at your own speed. They are the people that take what you are interested in and they work with that, to find some pretty great work experiences." Following her time with TTW, Reagh found employment working with the animals at Hennigar's Farm Market. She happily described her work placement there as "da bomb."

Her summer time work placement turned into long term employment. "You can look and look but I bet you will never find anyone who loves their job as much as I do." She went on to say that, "This is the dream job that I have been looking for all my life. Sometimes it feels like a really good dream, and I never want to wake up from it."

ARLENE MACASKILL: A PROFILE

Arlene McAskill was a former employment counsellor for PIE and she initiated contract discussions with Michelin in 1996. She made a proposal for employment opportunities at the Waterville plant for PIE clients. "In many ways, Arlene *is* the Michelin contract," says Tatlock. "She's the one that got it going."

"I remember being at those meetings and literally pounding the table and saying, 'If they don't tell you to F-Off, go back!' That's a hard assignment," Tatlock admits, but "Arlene was keeping contact with me about her progress."

McAskill designed and presented a proposal for employment opportunities at the Waterville plant in 1996. Soon after she resigned from The Flower Cart and relocated to the city, but the foundation had been laid.

Following Arlene's departure, the proposal lay dormant until she was replaced by Lisa Hammet-Vaughan, the job developer at PIE. It was her task to re-establish the lines of communication with Michelin and carry the project forward.

Her first priority was to follow up on the groundwork done by Arlene and she would soon take the Michelin relationship to a whole new level. "I was introduced to the spirited personality of Terry Dean who was the Area Personnel Manager," she recalls. "He told me with conviction, 'I am going to make this happen.'

After that initial meeting I called him numerous times to say, what about this idea? And what about that possibility? We finally got to a point where I said, look, I've got some people who I think would be ready to come and I'd like to come and see exactly what you have there. This time we toured the whole plant and I filled a notepad, writing down so many different ideas. I remember coming away from there so excited because there were lots of different opportunities."

The excitement was somewhat tempered by practicality as she tried to match the work to the trainee.

"I had to think about what we could really manage with the people that we had. What were the right jobs for them and where would they work best? What shops had the best supervision and support, because originally we thought we were going to just take people out there and leave them there.

We put three men out there to begin with. I supervised from afar for a while but at the end of the first year they said they wanted someone to supervise on site. It was a different model, one that allowed them to take on more Flower Cart people."

One of the early challenges was educating Michelin about the breadth of intellectual disabilities and what expectations could reasonably be placed on each of the prospective employees. Misconceptions had to be dealt with, rules had to be written, and concerns addressed as they arose. It was a period of adjustment for both sides.

"The supervision extended beyond their work at Michelin and into their private lives," says Hammett-Vaughn. "At first I think Michelin had been picturing people that were quite severely handicapped and they didn't really understand the spectrum, from severe to moderate. They had no idea how close to a regular worker someone with a handicap can be."

The leverage and credibility that accompanied the Michelin contract could not be overestimated. Tatlock views it as a culmination of years of hard work and perseverance in identifying and courting potential Annapolis Valley employers. In a larger sense, it was the result of following the original vision of providing work with purpose.

The value of the 1998-99 contract was a modest $49,000, but it marked a significant breakthrough in efforts to place workers. The work that had been done by trainers and staff was validated.

The original work was rubber stripping - peeling different types of rubber apart to reclaim it so that it could be put back in the production process. In August the official contract for labour services was signed. By October one of the workers was reassigned to another shop in the plant to perform a different task. The partnership was well and truly established and although there would be growing pains and setbacks, the goal of providing work with purpose had been met.

Once established, the job opportunities continued to grow. Some were temporary, others long-term, and in 2000, a Contract Administrator was hired to supervise the full-time employees. The following year a downturn in the tire industry led to the temporary layoff of all five Flower Cart employees. By Michelin's request, the contract was kept open by having someone continue to wash company cars, and when the industry recovered, the clients were immediately re-employed.

"It was like we never missed a beat," recalls Lisa Hammett Vaughn. "More job opportunities were identified and the number of workers continued to grow. I recall Terry Dean saying at one point before being transferred to a plant in Thailand, 'I think 10 is the maximum number of people you'll have in here.' "

In 2006, with 15 contract workers from the Flower Cart in Michelin Waterville, a Contract Administrator was once again hired. Jobs opened up in various areas of the plant and The Flower Cart was regularly asked to fill them.

"The morale boost that it gave us was priceless," recalls Tatlock. "I was at a meeting and the Michelin representative told us, 'We can't make a tire without The Flower Cart, not one single tire.' Those were his exact words. Can you imagine what that meant to us? The impact on our group was dramatic."

"Just imagine that. Their tires are in the top three of all exports in the province of Nova Scotia and they can't do it without us. That's something to be excited about! When you walk into a start-up or into an established business and they say 'Flower Cart? Handicapped people? Sorry, there's no place for you here.' We can look them in the eye and say, 'Well, we've got a place at Michelin, the third biggest exporter in NS.' "

Lisa Hammett-Vaughn looks back at those days with both satisfaction and pride. "I wish I could talk to Terry Dean in person about the history of our partnership with Michelin," she says. "I know that one of the first things I would say to him, with a smile on my face and gleam in my eye, would be, 'A maximum of ten, eh?'"

Since July of 1998, The Flower Cart has provided regular contract labour to the Michelin plant in Waterville, NS. The number of positions has grown steadily over the years and they served over 40 contract workers in 2019-20. The Flower Cart Michelin Contract

Workers (MCWs) now perform duties relating to rubber recovery, knife and scissor sharpening, machine cleaning, and inventory control and stocking.

CRAIG BUGDEN, A PROFILE

One of the original Michelin contract workers was Craig Bugden who began work there in the summer of 1998. In 2020, he's still a valued, reliable employee. During those years he has shown his versatility, performing any job that was asked of him, from knife sharpening to rubber recovery. For the last several years, he's worked primarily in a shop called OPX assisting with preparation work for article builders. Jim Rose, the OPX Business Unit Leader and Craig's Michelin supervisor is effusive in his praise of Bugden.

"Craig is a fantastic worker," he said in recognition of Craig's 20th anniversary. "I wish I had two or three more of him. When he goes on vacation it takes a couple of people to take his place." Craig's Michelin Contract Coordinator, Matt Clairmont, presented Craig with a 20th Anniversary plaque to recognize his unique contribution to the partnership. "Over the years, Michelin has noticed the great work he does and they've asked us to bring more people to fill other jobs," says Clairmont. "That's how we went from a couple of contract workers in those days to over 40 positions."

In 2008, on his tenth anniversary as an employee, Craig was asked to look back to his hiring and describe what the job has meant to him. "One thing the job means to me is better wages," he began, "but even more is that I feel like I really fit in this place. I am treated as an equal, not as an inferior. In my past couple of jobs… people put me down. Here they don't."

Craig was impressed with the Michelin rules about not tolerating discrimination. "Here I feel safe," he said. "Anyone who judges others on what type of jobs they do or what school they went to, they're losers."

Gay Clarke was Craig's supervisor as the Contract Coordinator and has several fond memories, but one in particular that still brings a smile to her face.

"There was a certain type of knife that was needed to cut certain angles on the rubber, and two parts that you had to sharpen. One day the Vice President of Marketing for Michelin North America was touring the plant and he visited the knife shop.

When the visitor came in I just left them alone and let them talk to whoever they wanted. He went over and started talking to Craig. He looked at the job Craig was doing and commented that it looked hard to do. Craig looked away from his work and up at the man, and never missed a beat. 'You got to be at one with the steel,' he said, ever so coolly.

I loved it. The man just smiled and walked away. He came to me and told me the story and said he really wanted to laugh. I said, 'then laugh!'."

The quid pro quo is obvious. Michelin gets dedicated, well-trained workers and The Flower Cart gets meaningful, challenging employment in a major production environment. The contract workers have a chance to develop life and work skills with an on-site support staff to ensure they are successful.

"Our contract has served both organizations well," says Clairmont. "To have this kind of unique, large scale partnership and to make opportunities for so many people, that is something to be celebrated."

The relationship is built on mutual respect and mutual need and practicality. It's a genuine partnership and those who think it was done solely as a gesture of corporate goodwill are mistaken.

"Michelin have their own way of doing things and it's not just being a good corporate citizen thing," says Tatlock. "They told us upfront that we had to prove ourselves to them, that they were not going to give us the keys to the plant."

"More importantly, they were concerned about the structure through which we would supervise and maintain the employees with intellectual disabilities, because Michelin didn't supervise their own people as much as we did. Just the other day, I ran into a man who did supervise some of our people. He had since retired but he was very proud of the work they had done. He couldn't wait to talk to me about the time he had The Flower Cart employee and how well it had worked out."

"I'd be in tears if I started telling you stories because it really is the very tip of the iceberg. I could show you the chart value of the Michelin contracts year over year and you could see what's going on. I'd show it to our board and I'd go out and make presentations and point to it and say, 'Well, the contract started this year and just look at the value now.' But the Michelin contract went well beyond that alone. It opened so many doors. More importantly, the number of jobs created continued to grow and even reached the point where one of The Flower Cart's clients who started as a contract employee was hired by Michelin. That's the barometer for measuring success."

"How good are you at supervising those people with intellectual disabilities? How good are you at training them? How amenable are they to the work environment? How successful will they be? What will their productivity be? Well, they hired one of them so there's your answer."

A LASTING PARTNERSHIP

Further evidence of the Michelin partnership, if needed can be found in the fact that The Flower Cart model has been incorporated into other locations and with other groups.

"The manager of the Michelin plant in Waterville was later sent to Rio de Janiero, and what was one of the first things he started on his watch?," says Tatlock. "A program like The Flower Cart for people that were living in Rio de Janeiro. Is that a paradigm shift? He was a good man."

"Here's a story about Michelin that I love," recalls Tatlock. "It's the weekend. Who works on the weekend? Grunts work on the weekend. Where are the supervisors? They're all in bed. So, our workers are doing tire verification, working on the tires as they slide down off the conveyor belt. We check on the tires. It's the middle of the night and a tire comes. Our Flower Cart worker, doing his job, looks at the tire. Tires are a bunch of rubbers all glued together and then baked. So he's looking at the laminate of the tire and thinks, 'There's something wrong with this tire.' He goes to the supervisor and shows him. The supervisor says, 'No that's alright.' Does he take that person's opinion, or does he know his job? He goes and finds that guy's supervisor in the middle of the night, in the plant and says, 'Look, there's something wrong with this tire." The supervisor's supervisor comes and looks at the tire, looks at the guy and yells, 'Shut her down! There's something wrong.'

That employee was given a certificate. I'm not going to say how much money that employee saved that plant but I'm telling you I didn't make that much money in my entire life, and my children and my entire family will never make as much money as that man saved that plant. He went to the supervisor, the supervisor said go back to work. But he knew his job was to verify and to ensure and he knew that 'oh, my god, if this goes through that's wrong. That is my job.'

How many non-handicapped people would just go back to work and just blame it on the supervisor? That was a clear indication of our worth to them. When that story was told to me, I was pounding the table that day, I'll tell you. That was so exciting!"

Since that initial contract, the Waterville Michelin work has become a mainstay for The Flower Cart. There have been obstacles along the way but none that couldn't be worked out by people of good will on both sides.

By 2005-2006, revenue from yearly Michelin contracts had grown from $49,000 to $250,000. By 2007-08 it had reached the $600,000 mark and in 2010-11, they topped the million-dollar plateau. There have been ups and downs, but this partnership has employed hundreds of contract workers who wouldn't have otherwise had an opportunity for such meaningful employment.

Hammett-Vaughn is justifiably proud of the Michelin breakthrough and not surprisingly she uses the identical phrase used by Roger Tatlock.

"They couldn't make a tire out here without The Flower Cart. I can think of times when our guys spotted problems in a way that nobody else did. Vinola (Robicheau) was one of the cases. She wasn't there at the plant, but she sewed elastics for them and she handled the stuff every day. They would provide these big industrial elastics, like you would have elastic in the waistband of a skirt and they're cut to length. They didn't want people to handle them within the plant, they wanted it as clean as possible. Vinola and her team were sewing them up to make them into a big elastic band and they used them throughout the plant and they have big spools or bobbins. Different color elastics tell them what material is on there, so one day Vinola was saying, 'this is not the same elastic'. I called up the guy who provided it and said it was different material. And he said, 'oh no, this is the same supplier, same lot number'. I said, 'my girl is telling me it's not the same and I'm just letting you know'.

Within a week he called me back and told me 'one of those elastics broke and it's not on the seam, it's not where your people sewed it, it's the material', and I said, 'well, what did my people tell you?' They could just feel the difference they'd handled it so often they knew it was a different quality."

Matt Clairmont has been the Michelin Contract Coordinator since August 2014 and while he's been responsible for continual growth, he recognizes there are still steps to be made.

"There are a lot of challenges involved in attempting to live up to The Flower Cart philosophy inside the Michelin environment," Clairmont says. "When I started I was really worried about being too directive and pushing too hard. Our organization puts the needs of the participants first and foremost, and I always remembered that, even in a major manufacturing environment.

What I noticed, however, was that our MCWs really responded to respect, empowerment, and clear expectations. Every time Michelin challenges us with a special project or a specific target, our team rises to the occasion.

We continue to have people like Craig Bugden who will likely continue in our program until they retire, and then we have more transitional workers, three of whom have in recent years been hired by Michelin. Both of those cases are examples of how we define the success of our program."

WHAT IS SUPPORTED EMPLOYMENT?

The term Supported Employment has been used by many organizations in the field of disability supports for decades but what does it really mean?

Supported Employment is a solution for individuals capable of providing valuable labour services, but who, for some reason or another, lack the capacity to obtain or maintain employment without reasonable accommodations. The reason Supported Employment is such a difficult term to define is that it is highly individualized; program planning and implementation varies greatly from one person to another.

"The key concept that I've learned in my career is never do something for someone that they can do themselves," says Matt Clairmont. "The temptation can be to remove as many obstacles as you can in their path, but quite often you just need to facilitate an encouraging environment and you'll see them overcoming obstacles by themselves. Ultimately, we want to help people find their limits and focus on continued growth."

For some that growth might come from setting small goals like coming in on time every day for a week. For others they might have broader employment goals, training courses they would like to take, or jobs they would like to apply for. The Flower Cart meets people where they are, assists them in setting goals, and uses Supported Employment to promote lifelong learning.

"On a daily basis Supported Employment means building a rapport, getting to know the people on our team and being able to identify when something is not quite right," says Clairmont. "We work shoulder to shoulder with our participants and we get to know how they act and react. We recognize when they are 'off' and we intervene accordingly. For some that means giving them space and time to sort out how they're feeling, while others might need someone to talk to. Knowing the difference is the art of providing Supported Employment."

The Flower Cart has excelled at being able to support a diverse group of participants, many of whom have intellectual disabilities and a variety of other barriers to employment. It has become increasingly common for participants to present with mental health issues, but there can also be additional barriers such as ADHD, Autism, or personality disorders. In each case, support means paying more attention to the person and not the diagnosis.

"Labels are for cans," says Clairmont, "and I am by no means the first one to say that, but it's really true. When people apply to work in my program they can be sheepish about disclosing a problem or a diagnosis and worried that it will disqualify them from getting a job. It hasn't yet. In fact, I just throw it aside and say, 'Ok, so what *can* you do?'. We've often been the first ones in a person's life who have been more interested in their ability than their disability."

For many, Supported Employment is the difference between being on social assistance or having a full-time job that pays a competitive wage. In that way, society benefits from having a wider base of working people paying income tax and spending their wages in the community, instead of being a drain on social programs. The Flower Cart offers supports on a daily, ongoing basis that helps dozens of participants obtain and maintain their employment. Without these supports, most if not all of them would be out of work.

"I think that's what makes a career in this field so enticing," says Clairmont. "You never know what you will be dealing with each day. I've had days where I've had to provide informal counselling on relationships, or participants feeling particularly down or depressed. I've had to work on grounding exercises as they recover from a panic episode. I've also had others who have expressed a desire to self-harm, and I've followed a strict procedure on how to refer them to mental health resources.

And then there are other days where I get to share lighter moments with our team. We set challenges and find ways to make the work interesting. We keep a good sense of humour and it makes the day pass a lot faster. It can be difficult work, but having someone there sharing in the experience and trying to make it better can make a big difference."

Additionally, there's no expiration date for Supported Employment. Some may enter a program like the Michelin contract and use it for short-term skill development. They will work for a few months, learning to follow a regular work schedule, how to interact with others, and provide quality labour. They learn the importance of working safely and effectively, and once they build confidence and competence, they take those enhanced skills to other jobs in the community.

Others may require support to remain employed for the foreseeable future. The barriers they face are significant enough that they need regular interventions from support staff. The individualized nature of the program means that there is no single evaluation tool, but each participant brings their own goals and their individual progress is the measure of success.

Supported Employment, for this purpose, means whatever it takes to the get the job done. "One of my favourite stories," says Clairmont, "comes from the first year or two after I joined the

Michelin team. They had a special job for one of our workers that extended after their scheduled stop time. Our guy was willing to stay but he couldn't because he had to go home and let his dog out. After speaking to him we made a plan and I left the plant with his keys, drove to his home, and took his dog for a walk so he could stay and earn a couple hours of overtime. That's when I learned that Supported Employment can mean a pretty broad range of services."

GARY SANFORD: A PROFILE

Gary Sanford is, by his own admission, "old school". When he landed his career as a knife sharpener at the Larsen meat plant in Berwick, Nova Scotia, he did it the old-fashioned way. He didn't have a resume or references, he just made an appointment with the manager and told him he wanted a job.

"I told him I'd make him a deal," Gary says. "I told him I'd work one week for free, and if I did good work, he'd hire me. He didn't take the deal, but he liked the fact that I was willing to offer it. He knew how bad I wanted to work and all he said was, 'You start Monday'."

If things had gone as Gary planned that would be the end of the story. He did end up working for Larsen for thirty-three years and had every intention of riding out the remainder of his working years for the company famous for producing sliced meats, bacon, and ham products. He was good at his job, had good benefits and an understanding team, and he was devastated to learn that the plant was closing in April 2011.

"It changed everything," Gary admits. "I went from feeling like I was productive and doing my part for my family, to feeling like I wasn't a man. I didn't know what I was going to do, but I knew I didn't want to go on unemployment."

Unfortunately, the options for Gary were limited. Not only did the closure of the Larsen plant throw nearly 300 people out of work, but he also has a barrier to employment. Gary is illiterate, and even though this didn't disadvantage him in any meaningful way in over thirty years at work, it would keep most employers from taking his application seriously. For this first time since he walked into the manager's office and got hired, Gary was afraid for his future and his ability to provide for his family, so much so that he hadn't done any real job searching for fear of rejection.

About a month after the Larsen plant closed a neighbour mentioned The Flower Cart to Gary and explained that they had work out at the Michelin plant. "I thought, I have a mortgage, a wife, a son, and no job," he says. "I'm afraid of change but I've also survived a heart attack and cancer, so how bad can this be? I decided to go see what they were all about."

"I met with Gay Clarke at the Michelin Gatehouse and she went over the program. Everything was so different from what I was used to but I just needed a job. All I said was, 'when can I start?'"

To many, Gary's inability to read would disqualify him. To Gay and her team at Michelin, Gary was a knife sharpener and they had knives that needed to be sharpened. It was as simple as that, and for nearly ten years Gary Sanford worked diligently sharpening knives in the Michelin knife shop, the knives used every day in tire production.

"My mother was my rock," says Gary. "She taught me about the rule of three-one hundreds. Always give one hundred percent to your family, that's your first and greatest responsibility. Then, give one hundred percent to your employer, that's the only way you can get anywhere in life. Last, you have to give a hundred percent to yourself, take care of yourself and get your mindset correct so you can be the man you're supposed to be."

In March 2020 Gary and the rest of The Flower Cart Michelin team were forced off work due to another interruption, this one caused by Covid-19. "That was scary," he recalls, "getting the call that we had to stay home, hearing the Prime Minister tell

Canadians he hoped our jobs would come back. Eventually things started to get better and I heard that our team was allowed back into the plant, but not the knife sharpening crew. I was getting worried.

I started thinking, what if I don't get my job back? What then? My wife Teena knew it was bothering me and one day she just said, 'it's all about learning to adapt. You have a disability, you lost your job, you had other struggles, and every time we came out all right'. She was right."

Matt Clairmont had taken over the Michelin contract in 2014 and he was tasked, in June 2020, with leading the team back into the plant after a government-imposed suspension of Supported Employment activity in Nova Scotia was lifted. Slowly but surely the team returned, but there remained uncertainty with the knife shop that was now staffed by Michelin personnel. In order to get Gary a job he would have to start a different job and learn a new skill.

"When I got the call about coming back I was excited," says Gary, "until I heard it wouldn't be in the knife shop. But then I realized, I have obligations to my wife, to my son. I was angry because I didn't want to change, but I had to teach myself to adjust.

I haven't really thought about how life would be different for me without The Flower Cart. I know what it means to me and how it helps people. I also know that a lot of places would look at me and my disability and see me as a liability. It was never like that here."

Gary has since returned to work at the rubber recovery post. He has learned how to operate a stripping machine, and how to palletize and sort material. He gets some support from his team with labelling and reading product tags, but for the most part he's fine with coming in, getting to work, and doing a good job.

"Now I just have one goal. I want to get to 60 and then reduce to three days per week. After that? Who knows."

A FLOWER CART REUNION

In December of 2015 Carol Rafuse stopped in at the Flower Cart to pay a bill for bread. While she was waiting, a picture on the wall caught her eye. It was the photo of a participant celebrating 25-years of service to The Flower Cart. She examined it more closely and was startled to see how closely the person resembled her mother.

When she returned home later that day she contacted her sister Candace Bird and told her that she was fairly certain that the person in the picture was their long-lost sibling. They talked it over, trying to decide what to do. "I couldn't believe it," Bird told Wendy Elliott of *The Kings County News*. "Then we were concerned. We didn't want to upset the apple cart, but we wanted to meet her."

Machelle Hubley, the woman whose face Carol had recognized, was two years old when her mother Gwendolyn decided that her mentally- and physically-challenged daughter was too much for her to handle. It was then that Machelle became a ward of the province and her childhood was spent in a series of foster homes. She went on to attend the Nova Scotia Youth Training School in Truro and when L'Arche Homefires opened in Wolfville, she became the first female core member.

A meeting was arranged. "We needed to see her," said Bird. "We'd lost our dad a couple of years earlier. That left a large hole." Candace and Coral were under the mistaken impression that Machelle had been adopted and was living in another province but as the three sisters talked, they quickly realized that they had been living within a few miles of each other without knowing.

Machelle, the eldest of the three, was thrilled to be reunited with her two sisters after a separation of five decades. "I was nervous, excited and happy," she said. Rafuse says she fussed over her hair and make-up as if she were on a "first date." Once together, they were suddenly inseparable. After a celebration at Tim Hortons, they placed a phone call to their mother and when Machelle was handed the phone, her first words were, "Hi, Mom."

The call was followed by a face-to-face meeting with her mother and 90-year old grandmother, making Christmas 2015 a genuine family affair. "It's a great, great story about gifts you can't buy in the store, all thanks to The Flower Cart.

THE END OF THE ROAD

Roger Tatlock has an imposing athlete's bearing to go with his close-cropped hair and intensity. You don't have to be in his presence long before you know that he's a fierce competitor and goal-oriented team player. He has a game plan and sticks to it. He also has a determined will to win.

"When you think about what this book is," says Tatlock, "to me it's a summation, it's definitely a celebration, and it's a passing. First fifty years, look how much we've done! Now, what are the goals for the next fifty?

People ask me, Roger, why did you retire? I say look, social change is hard. It sucked the marrow out of my bones, it's something you do every single day. People used to say to me: you work all the time. I'd say there's only a couple of times in my life when I don't think about The Flower Cart.

There were no laptop computers then. I'd pack up my CPU on a Friday night, take it home, sit there in my living room with the computer doing budgets and not knowing how to devise cash flows and pulling my hair out. But I didn't regret one minute of that, because when you're involved in social change and that's what you're doing, it's not a nine to five job.

Fifty years is cause for celebration but also for passing on of the torch. The Flower Cart was something of a guiding light for the province in terms of showing the way. It was also a bit of a light in that all the moths came to us – by which I mean the good people. Not just good in terms of good at their job but good in their heart, in the way that they thought about the world.

Jim Oulton, what he did, and Joanne Porter, what she did — changing society and thinking about how society could be better by embracing diverse populations and diverse people, and seeing that diverse people have their place in your neighbourhood, in your society. People don't think like that normally. They think about paying their bills and raising their kids and keeping the wolf from the door.

And when I think of Jim and Joanne and Catherine Lowe and Debbie Gainey, Marlene Dodge in her quiet way— spending her whole work life like that. Just imagine, an innocent teenager working in an institution like Mountain View and then coming to The Flower Cart and realizing, 'I'm going to work the rest of my life because things are happening here that fit with how people should be treated'. Or Kevin West, working in the trenches every day, building things, solving problems..."

After 21 years as executive director, Roger Tatlock submitted his resignation in the last quarter of the 2013-2014 fiscal year. At the time of his leaving, The Flower Cart served 280 clients and 83 were employed in the community at minimum wage or more. In his 22 years as executive director, Roger Tatlock saw The Flower Cart grow and prosper. He introduced many programming innovations and oversaw countless success stories, financial and social, big and small, but when asked what he considers the most significant development during his tenure, he doesn't hesitate.

"If I had to point to one thing I'm most proud of in my time as director, I'd say the growth of social enterprise," says Tatlock. He doesn't stop there, suggesting that social enterprise was responsible for the financial viability and overall independence of the charitable enterprise. "The year that the percentage of The Flower Cart revenue went to 51% self-generated, I was pretty proud."

Yet his concern is that the mission goes before the money, and he thinks of his experience with the bakery for a concrete example. "We learned a lot about social enterprise from our experience with the bakery. When they first hired a baker, he ran it as the prince of that bakery and all the people ran around him. That was the model - and then they changed the model. They said, 'no, we're going to hire a few human service people and make sure that they can bake and learn the baking – but the human service should come first'.

"It's the baking that enables the human service *not* the human service fitting into the bakery. The board needs a lot of credit for the evolution – for the baby steps that were taken back then and also the self-awareness to decide that they were not going to do it the same way they'd always done it. They pivoted to 'We need the bakery to serve clients, not the clients to serve the bakery.' "

With his dogged determination and faith in the value of work, Roger Tatlock left The Flower Cart a stronger, larger, and more impactful organization than he found it, and prepared it for the next steps in an ambitious evolution.

CHAPTER SIX: EXPANSION

Jeff Kelly joined The Flower Cart on May 12, 2014 and social enterprise continued to be a top priority. Included in the list of such enterprises were Just Us! Coffee Roasters Co-Op, Omega Crunch, and Michelin as well as Blomidon Nurseries, a new partner for employment experience.

There were also more immediate challenges. Cost-saving measures by Michelin led to a restructuring of the employment contract. As a result nearly half of the workforce were laid off in December 2014, and even with the layoffs The Flower Cart suffered its worse fiscal year in its history and were forced to re-open the Michelin contract and negotiate more favourable terms.

It was far from all bad news, however. Kelly had the pleasure of accepting an Ethics Award from Better Business Bureau Atlantic. The Scotiabank-sponsored award celebrated Atlantic Canadian businesses and The Flower Cart was nominated in the non-profit category. Kelly summed up the message the award expressed, stating matter-of-factly, "Doing the right thing the right way is how we operate."

His first months on the job were spent learning about the various social enterprise activities and getting to know the staff and participants. "I am continually reminded that having an intellectual disability as a barrier to employment can be broken down with the right accommodations and supports," he says. "Our participants leave at the end of the day feeling a sense of accomplishment for a job well done, just as any other worker does at the end of a productive day."

A top priority was finding a new location for the vocational and pre-vocational programs, as well as a home for the expanded list of new products and services that The Flower Cart will be providing. A property that had been purchased at 9503 Commercial Street in 2013 was still seen as a possible new site for constructing a new building and in the spring of 2015 a draft conceptual design was received from the architect. Estimated cost for the new facility was $4 million. Another option under consideration was purchasing the former Zeller's building in the County Fair Mall and repurposing it.

Due to the contract setbacks The Flower Cart had experienced a poor financial report for 2013-2014. The end of Kelly's first year showed a return to financial health with the social enterprises once again flourishing and long-time service contracts stabilized.

The Social Enterprise Council of Canada provided a definition of social enterprise, calling it "businesses owned by non-profit organizations, that are directly involved in the production and/or selling of goods and services for the blended purpose of generating income and achieving social, cultural, and/or environmental aims." They go on to say, "Social enterprises are one more tool for non-profits to use to meet their mission to contribute to healthy communities."

The Nova Scotia Social Enterprise Working Group adds that "all profits are reinvested to support community needs." Kelly likes to keep it simple. To him, social enterprise is "capitalism with purpose". Everything The Flower Cart creates, fresh baked bread, picnic tables, washer toss games; these are all products of social enterprise.

The concept was about to get a boost from a highly anticipated report commissioned by the Nova Scotia government. With the release of the One Nova Scotia Report, *Now or Never: An Urgent Call to Action for Nova Scotians*, also known as the Ivany Report, The Flower Cart's business activities received provincial attention. The report recognized social enterprise as a key driver for economic development in the province, especially in rural areas, and The Flower Cart is singled out as a leader and an example of best practices in social enterprise development.

The Flower Cart had been evolving as a social enterprise over many years. It had now become a conglomerate of social enterprises. An entrepreneurial spirit had spread throughout the organization and manifested itself in a variety of products and services. The eclectic array of activity was designed to serve emerging markets and to meet the needs of a wide range of participants

The foundation was solid. It was time to build on past successes and become a serious player in the business community. The Flower Cart seemed to be taking its rallying cry directly from the pages of the Ivany Report: "The only certainty is that the status quo is not an option."

There would be no resting on laurels under the new administration. They had learned much from the successes and failures of past ventures. It was time to expand the range of social enterprises and bring projects to the next level.

The bakery had been The Flower Cart's first foray into social enterprise and Kelly, whose office was directly above the bakery, was reminded of that daily as the aroma of warm bread and rolls permeated the air. It was the smell of success and an enticement to add to the list of social enterprises. "We've been successful in our baking operation, woodworking, packaging and labeling as well as general contract labour services," Kelly wrote in his first annual report. "They are all social enterprises in Kings County that help achieve our mission."

THE BUSINESS MODEL

When Roger Tatlock retired as director in April of 2014 and Kelly took over the reins in May, there were inevitable changes in style and approach. Like Tatlock, Kelly is a firm believer that the driving force for the organization is the work and much of that work is social enterprise. Like The Flower Cart itself, the social enterprise concept has evolved to meet the demands of a changing society.

With the growing emphasis on work comes an increased emphasis on fair compensation for that work. The challenge is to reconcile fair pay into the equation while maintaining the spirit and substance of social enterprise. In addition, the most up-to-date criteria for social enterprise includes the need for the voices of the participants to be heard. They should also have a say in the design process for the enterprise and community-industry partnerships must be fostered. Kelly is moving ahead on all those fronts.

"I think there has been some evolution to it," he says. "My predecessors built on the core principle of what was cited as the mission of the organization. It has remained pretty close to what its original founders envisioned it to be and I certainly am an ardent proponent of that through support of employment, vocational training opportunities, and collaboration with other service providers. We're essentially just going to continue to do that but it's going to focus on the participants.

"It'll be participant-led with respect to identification of what other types of opportunities they'd like to explore. For example, let's say the group says they want to do yoga, we will try to incorporate a yoga opportunity for them. We will support our people when they express an interest in something."

The importance of meaningful, purposeful employment remains, but the employment has taken on a new imperative.

"I'm absolutely, 100% behind what Roger (Tatlock) says about the importance of work," says Kelly. "I think the evolution in society right now is yes, work is still great for this population, but it's also a human rights issue. If they're working, they need to be compensated fairly. I'm a firm believer in that. If they're working in the co-packing kitchen they will be paid to do that. We've made the business case for that and will continue the practice, and it's the same with the bakery.

That's where the evolution is occurring. It's already happened in other jurisdictions and its eventually going to be required here. The Flower Cart, at its root, has always been focused on quality work activity. That has been fantastic and has established The Flower Cart as a leader within adult day program services providers for decades.

Right now, about 39% of our participants earn minimum wage or better. A sizeable chunk of that is Michelin and in our processing facility down the street with our co-packing kitchen. All those folks are earning minimum wage and we're going to transition that into the bakery as the next step. To me that says we've reached a true level of social enterprise, that participants realize the value of the work they are doing, and that we respect what they bring to the organization. As with any worker anywhere in society, how do you show that respect, besides just telling them? You pay them!"

THE NEXT GENERATION

As The Flower Cart moves into a new facility and a new half-century of service, Kelly envisions an expanded role for social enterprise. "Where I'd like to see further evolution occur, and it's my own personal belief but it's also being very practical in respect to how the provincial government would like to see day programming evolve, is expansion of choice and opportunity for people.

"The location of the new facility, next door to the Louis Millett Complex, gives us an ideal opportunity to partner with the Village of New Minas to provide new opportunities as part of our core programming. The difference is that they won't necessarily be delivered in the facility that will be identified as a vocational training, supported employment centre."

The design of the new Flower Cart complex will allow participants to more fully realize the potential of social enterprise. "That's why our capital campaign was branded *Building Opportunities*," says Kelly. "It offers opportunities both within the new facility and outside in the greater community. We'll work with our neighbour in the Village of New Minas to promote more inclusive opportunities for social development. I'm not a huge fan of the recreation and leisure terminology because it conjures up images of folks coming to us to play badminton all day, but we are going to expand upon the opportunities that we already have incorporated as part of our program of options. It's always been a partnership."

When Kelly came in as executive director, there was a substantial change in the composition of the board of directors. "We brought in new people aligned with our vision," he says. "Social enterprise is now more rights-based. It's all about the human right to work with dignity and be paid for that work. It applies both in-house and in the community. Up to now, there was a wage and there was a stipend, depending on whether you were a worker or a trainee. Ultimately that will change so that all participants will be paid a wage. Roger used to say that it's the mission, not the money, but with no money, no mission."

As part of the changing dynamic, Kelly saw the need to rebrand The Flower Cart name to better showcase its collection of social enterprises.

"We rebranded in 2016 to become The Flower Cart Group. Adding that word 'Group' allowed us to start developing and promoting our enterprise brands. We now have those displayed on our communications material, and distinct logos will be in full view on the main signage at our new location. The signage will be more akin to what you see in a strip mall. It'll be brands on top with the parent group underneath."

"The social media campaign that we've had for the last few years has been building up recognition of The Flower Cart Group. We'll be more concerted in our effort to develop the Baker's Choice Fine Foods identity on its own. I think that demonstrating all the brands that we have within the Flower Cart Group also lends itself to more public recognition of the various opportunities that we offer participants, and that's really what it's all about. It's all about the opportunities."

The capital campaign is one of the most ambitious projects in the history of the organization, but Kelly is quick to point out that it "is actually about more than just the physical building that we're raising money to build. It's about the partnership."

"We can have stronger relationships with Kaleidoscope (a social recreation program for youth with special needs) and make use of the village's Louis Millett Complex to expand some opportunities. Lockhart-Ryan Park is just behind us. That offers opportunities as well. We've already done some of these things but on a very small, ad hoc scale because The Flower Cart has always been about work!"

"We're even revisiting our mission statement right now to make sure that it adequately contains all that we are. The mission statement from 1973 has gone through variations over five decades but it's always been supported training and employment, or variations of that. It's still very much a pillar of who we are and what we do, but I think it's also important to emphasize the other opportunities that we'll have available.

Personally, I'm excited about opportunities to do so much more and on a more frequent basis: even sign language classes for those who want to communicate with a colleague with hearing impairment. The community development and recreation coordinator for New Minas, John Ansara, is very excited at all the possibilities.

We have one deaf participant named Dennena who signs and a couple of staff are trained in sign language so they can communicate with her. But the colleagues who participate in the programs every day would like the opportunity to do some very basic communication with her as well. We now have our folks attend a sign language class a couple of hours a week in our current building but we'll now have the opportunity to actually go and use one of the community rooms at the Millett Complex to do that.

We could have a coordinated approach to the delivery of those classes and make use of one of those community rooms. We can probably have someone from the community come in and do the teaching.

It's this sort of opportunity that the Village of New Minas can support. It'll create a physical connection between our two campuses. It's a fantastic partnership and I'm really excited about it."

JEFF KELLY: A PROFILE

Every executive director arrives with a different well of experience. They take different routes, some direct and some winding, but they all arrive with different skill sets and past experiences, and different strengths. Some have backgrounds in education and others in social work. The one thing they have in common is a drive to help the people that are supported by the organization.

Kelly's professional background was unlike those of his predecessors and his journey to The Flower Cart was circuitous. Born in Saint John, New Brunswick, the son of a businessman and ECG technician, he moved to Bridgewater in 1985 where he attended Park View Education Centre. He joined the army in 1991 and served with the second regiment Royal Canadian Horse Artillery in Petawawa.

He left the army in 1994 and enrolled at St. Thomas University in Fredericton, majoring in political science. He transferred to St. Mary's University in Halifax and finished in 1998. His next stop was graduate school at Dalhousie University where he graduated in 2000 with a master's degree in public administration and worked in a graduate internship program in Winnipeg, Manitoba until 2004.

He subsequently worked at the Metro Food Bank in Halifax from 2004-06 during their rebrand to Feed Nova Scotia. He moved on to the NSCC Kingstec campus where he worked in the early childhood education program. He then became executive director of the NS Physiotherapy Association. It's an impressive and varied resume that has served him and his community well as he deals with the plethora of issues The Flower Cart faces.

Asked if his approach is guided by any philosophical guru in the field of intellectual disabilities as Wolfensberger guided Tatlock, Kelly freely acknowledges that he comes to the job from a different background and brings a different approach.

"I'd never worked with the population identified as intellectually disabled previously in any of my positions. But I have quite a lot of experience working in the non-profit area and come from a program administration background. I've gravitated to social enterprise and my vision is to model what an inclusive workplace should embody. As we bring folks in they're going to work in our social enterprises, they know they'll be treated with respect and dignity, they're being paid.

They will be confident that whatever levels of support that need to be accommodated are being provided within our various enterprises. We know that some folks may have barriers to full time work, or to the employment that we accommodate. Put in simple terms, we get the job done for our customers and we do it with a population that has traditionally been challenged to enter an employment position.

I don't really have the philosophical background of those that came before me. I'm more of a pragmatist, I guess – not to say being grounded in a philosophical direction isn't also pragmatic. I think we run businesses and provide as many opportunities, choices, and options as possible for the people that we support.

To even use the label of intellectually disabled right now is problematic and I rarely use it, I rarely talk about it. I use the word 'person' rather than participant. Obviously people know what The Flower Cart is and who goes there, but our doors are open to a lot of different types of individuals. Everybody is unique.

Everybody who comes to us for some support or program service, they may work within our vocational training areas and our community work experience opportunities for a while. Then they may transition to a community job, they may go and put some hours in our social enterprises, or any number of options. We're opening up many opportunities to folks so that they're not just able to work in one area of the organization.

There's going to be a variety. And the organization has had that for many years; I don't want to mislead you into thinking this is something new. What is new is the organizational structure around those opportunities. It's being included more in the culture and the public is going to see it. Like the new facility and how it's going to be designed, it's going to look more like a mini strip mall or a sort of industrial park. It will look like you're going into some businesses, whether you go into the bakery to pick up an order or you go into our newest enterprise, a co-working space called Bloom.

Bloom is an exciting part of our future. We'll be able to bring in members of the community and encourage collaboration. Our participants will work in Bloom and be included in the running of the business itself."

Bloom is The Flower Cart's first foray into the emerging business of coworking, and they see a lot of potential in incorporating a community hub in the design of the new facility. "It's a space where folks that are entrepreneurs with home offices or businesses can come in and buy memberships to basically rent a work space. It's a space to have small meetings, presentations, and events. There are independent office spaces included within the design, so if you want to take a private meeting with one of your clients or customers, there's space available.

Kelly gets excited when discussing the potential for the workspace. "There's a board room attached to it too, a large floor rental space with a coffee bar set up. We want to build community capacity before we launch this new enterprise so we'll go out to the community and ask what they want within this space, because that's who our customers are going to be. Our people are going to be in charge of them coming in, making sure the space is clean and stocked with coffee and that snacks are available. Ideally, we'd like to support our local entrepreneurs, and we want them to support us, too."

"The key to these spaces is flexibility of use. Most people who come to these kind of places have their own equipment. They just need the space. It's just going to be tables that can be moved around, the people, and what they bring to the community hub, is what makes it special.

You may be working on a project and the person next to you happens to be a graphic designer. They may lean over and say, 'I've got an idea'. These are the kinds of synergies that you get from working next to people who are working on similar goals. Going to a coffee shop is fine, but it's just socialization for its own sake. Bloom is going to be our attempt at building our own little community.

And in the What's Cooking? Commercial Kitchen and Co-pack, there will be folks working in there consistently on contracts we have with Made with Local, Just Us! Coffee Roasters Co-Op, Farmer John's, and others. We have the flexibility to take on smaller customers and there aren't very many co-packers in this province that can do that. There are large co-packers where you need thousands upon thousands of units being run on a consistent basis, even daily, in order to justify the expense of going into a co-pack. We're going to be the answer for the little folks.

We're not profit-driven, however I do make it a point that our enterprises cannot lose money. At minimum they have to break even but I'm pushing for a contributions level, even if they are minor contributions. Now when Bloom gets started, we've budgeted that we're not going to see a contribution likely in that operation for a couple of years, as with any normal business start-up, you experience issues.

It's interesting to note how much of The Flower Cart revenues now comes from our own revenues versus government and other sources. It tends to fluctuate but we were 56% the last time I reported to the Board. That's revenue generated from social enterprise after we pay our contract workers real wages. The remainder is then invested into the overall operating costs of the operation.

And the various outlets in the new facility, including Bloom, will offer wage-paying opportunities for the participants as well as generating positive contributions back to the organization itself."

Even with all those ambitious projects getting started, the biggest challenge for Kelly was the Michelin contract, and negotiating it so that it worked for future growth. "It was a significant bump in the road, but the big take away about the Michelin experience is 21 years with them wanting to provide opportunities for our program to grow within that plant. That's a great thing."

"The scale and scope of our contract, and the costs associated with it, put us on a level where we compete with other contractors, and I don't mind that. To me that's an evolution and that's a positive. We can go in and prove our worth, our value to the plant. Every day we get a chance to show what we can do and why we should be compensated appropriately, just like anybody else.

My first year negotiating with Michelin was tough because I came into a situation where the contract that we had signed would be detrimental to the organization if it continued any longer. There were some hardball tactics on both sides of the fence, and we had to make something that worked for everyone. Ultimately, I'm happy that we got a contract that was feasible for us.

Our job totals at Michelin have been as high as 75, but we're now at about 40. That's a good, sustainable number. Any more and we find it creates challenges for our support team. I've scaled back the number of support people that could be out there. We have a coordinator and a team of two out supportive coworkers out there. Most of their job is dealing with the human service challenges that our clients bring to the workplace. Our folks all have skills; they can do the jobs that they're asked to do. It's been the other things that can prevent any of them from being successful at previous employment opportunities.

What makes that work particularly interesting is how broad the supports are that you can offer. One contract worker might just need a little help reading product sheets, for instance. Others might need strict coaching on how to speak with their teammates. One worker might want help with job searches and resumes, and another might need advice on a deeply personal matter. The support is holistic and informed, and it helps the team run smoothly."

PARTICIPANT PLANNING GROUP

Another evolution under Kelly's leadership has been the formation of the Participant Planning Group and its first meeting in November 2018.

"It's an updated iteration of what would have happened at the Workers' Councils in the eighties and nineties with Joanne (Porter) and Jim (Oulton)," says Kelly. "The Participant Planning Group is just focused on running these meetings per se and identifying issues that they would like addressed and talked about at the meetings."

The current planning group is made up of nine participants who have an opportunity to discuss issues that impact their lives and work. It's the responsibility of the members themselves to identify the issues they would like addressed and draw up the agenda for the monthly meetings. Each group member is asked to present an agenda item for discussion.

"I ran the meetings at first but not anymore," says Kelly. "For the most part, the meetings are now run by the participants themselves. They have evolved into what we like to call co-hosts. There would usually be a staff person present along with one of the participants to co-chair, or co-host, the meeting. As for me and my report, I'm just a standing agenda item. I come in and I do my report to them."

In addition to the Executive Director's report, typical agenda items include Occupational Health and Safety updates, and reports from People First Kings County. The Participant Planning Group represents all Flower Cart participants and gives them a voice at the meeting. "Participants are aware of who is in the Participant Planning Group and can bring forward ideas through them so that they can be added to the agenda," says Kelly. "The meetings themselves are open to all participants. They're styled and run akin to a traditional staff meeting."

"The process empowers participants to speak their minds and thereby build confidence and self-advocacy skills. In addition, it helps to enhance the sense of community within The Flower Cart."

BUILDING OPPORTUNITIES

In 2020 The Flower Cart reached the halfway point of a major capital campaign to build a new facility. It is clearly the most ambitious project ever undertaken in its fifty-year history, and it has potential to be an enduring symbol of how far The Flower Cart has come.

From the moment Jeff Kelly was named Executive Director of The Flower Cart he understood that the current facility was outdated, ill-equipped, and too expensive to maintain. While the organization had made investments in property and had been in the pre-launch mode of a campaign for several years, Kelly's arrival kicked the project into gear.

"The capital campaign is co-chaired by Paul, my current board chair, who actually has a really interesting story. He relocated here from the city after a long career on the civilian side of the Department of National Defense as an electrical technologist. He worked mostly on submarines throughout his career. He has two children, Victoria and Philip, that are on the autism spectrum, and his wife Donna created the Kaleidoscope program.

Originally from Newfoundland, Paul Randell has brought a new perspective to The Flower Cart. "My background is more technical than it is in organizational," he says, "but over that period of time I was involved in various management positions and levels so I had an understanding about organizations and how things should or could operate. The military was very structured, and I think I bring some of that to The Flower Cart."

"When we lived in Halifax, we made many trips to the Annapolis Valley over the years. It was one our favourite weekend trips. In terms of our family situation, The Flower Cart was certainly a consideration in deciding to move here. Donna and I have two adult children with autism, so wherever we were going we needed to know there was something that would open doors for them and give them opportunities to have fulfilling days. Everyone needs purpose, so that was one of the key considerations.

We explored every option along the way, but The Flower Cart seemed to offer the most to meet our kids' needs. We decided we needed to be somewhere close and our youngest was still attending high school, so he started at Horton. The learning centre resource teacher, Gerald MacPherson, was on the board of The Flower Cart. Gerald worked hard to make the transition from one school to another pretty smooth and seamless for us. He's the one that introduced both my wife and me to The Flower Cart and now we're both on the board.

Phillip is our youngest child and Victoria is our middle daughter and they both have had an autism diagnosis. We also have an older daughter who's married and has her own family. Victoria and Philip's needs were paramount for us in moving but the move was meant to be something good for all of us.

To be quite honest, the different pace of life in the Annapolis Valley was a factor. It was a different climate in the sense that there seems to be with the SMILE program run out of Acadia and so on. People in the Annapolis Valley just seem to be a little more sensitive to people with disabilities, and more patient and understanding, at least in our experience.

Victoria is 28 and a full-timer at The Flower Cart. She goes every morning and works a full day, five days a week and she loves it. She loves knowing she has a place to go, a reason to get up and go every morning. She doesn't say a whole lot about it, but I think in her way it has become a purpose and it allows her to have more social interactions.

Once people with disabilities leave school there's a big void and if you're not going to some place like the Flower Cart, maintaining your connections is a real challenge. When we came here all the friends that Victoria grew up and went to school with were no longer close by. The Flower Cart really helped in that regard.

My son Philip is 26 years old and his needs are much different, so he participates at The Flower Cart in a different fashion. He does tasks once or twice a week for a very short time. Philip doesn't stay as focused as Victoria for as long; he likes to be in constant motion all the time. Naturally, it's more challenging for him to be in a group environment, but as we work with him things will improve.

My wife Donna is one of the founding members of a group called Kaleidoscope. It's a social recreational program run through the Village of New Minas and it fills a gap for lots of people. We have some people who have aged out of The Flower Cart more or less. Their physical abilities are reduced but they like the social part. That social aspect was key for people to keep connections with their community.

Jeff is a very progressive director. So is the entire board, actually, and once I became chair we did a whole new strategic plan. It was far more comprehensive or extensive than had been done previously. We really focused on creating opportunities and giving our participants the opportunities to make choices. Jeff and his staff have been amazing at incorporating that and nurturing that."

As a co-chair of the capital campaign Randell has been working diligently on the plan for procuring funds for the new facility. He and Kelly have been working closely and Randell has been impressed with his approach to this task.

"I don't know what we'd do without him. It was an awful big ask for someone that was fairly new in that position to just jump into that. I think in large part, the reason I took the job as chair and campaign co-chair was to provide that source of support for him. I was there and could commit for a fairly long period of time where most people would maybe be prepared to serve one or two years.

We don't typically go through a wholesale change-out with the board. There's a rotational schedule where people do a two- or three-year term to a maximum of seven years service. The year my wife and I joined there were seven new board members out of twelve, which was a significant change from the usual. But Jeff nurtured us through the learning phase and we seemed to function very well as a board. I have amazing individuals on that board, and the skills and experience they bring is awesome. We're very well placed to do great things."

RACHEL DURNO-ALLEN, A PROFILE

Rachel Durno-Allen was diagnosed with ADHD and also suffers with anxiety and depression. After completing high school she moved from Ontario to the Annapolis Valley and attempted to find work. Despite her many attempts, her specific needs always proved to be a roadblock to suitable employment. It was during this period of greatest frustration that The Flower Cart offered a solution.

"I tried almost everything," she says. "All the available jobs were too fast-paced for me — fast food, selling clothes, stocking shelves, hotel cleaning, farm work. I also discovered that if you don't know the right people, you don't get jobs."

"I always had dream jobs but none were realistically achievable for me, and that was something that did upset me — the fact that I couldn't do the 'normal jobs' like retail and fast food, but I also couldn't do my 'dream jobs.' I felt lost, like I could never be what society would deem a responsible hard working adult. I had the feeling of always being young and not able to reach my potential."

It was at this low point that Rachel was introduced to a counsellor at Partners in Employment, an agency of The Flower Cart Group.

"When I first heard of The Flower Cart, I thought it was a flower shop and I hate bugs so I figured it wasn't for me. I had also heard that it was only for certain people with major disabilities. Then I checked it out.

Previously when I'd gone to other employment places and told them what I can't do, they still put me in those environments. Once they placed me at a pharmacy where I'd have to be around people while stocking shelves and doing other tasks. So when Donna said, 'Here's an idea', I said, 'Oh, that actually sounds like you listened to me.'

That's when she led me to Family 1st Medical in New Minas and I met the manager, Kimberley Monette. I was nervous of course but after I got in there and they showed me what to do, I thought, this is a great job. I love this. I can put on my headphones, I can do my job, and I can see the finished product. A lot of times with work you don't get to see that — you just work and then go home but with this I can see when the tanks are clean. I can see the difference I'm making.

Family 1st has amazing people. The atmosphere is unlike all the other jobs I've had. I feel so calm going in every day. It wasn't, 'Oh another day of work,' or 'Oh the boss is coming.' I immediately loved it there. People were so friendly and open. At Family 1st I found respect. Obviously a boss — like a parent — isn't meant to be a friend but you still want that mutual connection of respect. In other jobs it was like they wanted you to be robotic, to do the job regardless of what else was going on and just do as they say.

In my case, I prefer to have headphones on and listen to You Tube while I work. They allow that to happen because they understand that turns around and makes me a more efficient worker. Just knowing that if there's something I can't do, they're not going to be negative about it, is such a change. They say, 'Well ok, what can we do to make it so that you can do that?'

Self-confidence was definitely something I suffered with and this job has given me more than a paycheck, it's given me self-confidence, a sense of achievement, and a feeling of being a team member. Some might see it as just scrubbing tanks, but I see it as giving a little bit of sparkle to something others might just view as a necessity for everyday use.

Since finding Family 1st I now feel like I have responsibility, purpose, and a reason to work hard. Now when someone asks what I do I can be proud of my answer."

Rachel's shining personality and work ethic prompted her manager to nominate her for the Biggs Award, presented annually to an outstanding Flower Cart participant employed in the community. To her surprise and delight, Rachel won the award for 2019.

"Honestly, I didn't know about the award and when I was first told, I went outside and I cried. Then I called my dad. It was very overwhelming to be recognized for my work. I thought I was just doing my job.

That's why The Flower Cart plays such an important role. There are so many people out there who just haven't found their spot and they just don't fall into the right category for some jobs. There needs to be more recognition for low income or low education people – or even people who have high education but can't to go to college. They can't seem to quite get there and so they need to be shown more suitable employment opportunities.

The big thing about The Flower Cart is that it works. I'd advise people to check it out. Just take the chance. Realize that everybody can do something. It's like the old commercial that we used to see on Canadian TV: Not everybody is good at everything, but everybody is good at something. Ignore the stigma, get out and give it a try. You'll be surprised at what's out there for opportunities.

It's changed my life so much. I was miserable knowing that I was not going to be able to work. I couldn't handle flipping burgers, I can't go to university and become a lawyer, although I wanted to. Now I have a job. I've moved to New Minas, I have an opportunity, a reason to get out of bed and go to work every day."

Kimberley Monette, general manager of Family 1st Medical sees community employment as mutually beneficial to clients and employers alike.

"In April 2018 Family 1st Medical New Minas had a need – find someone to make sure our oxygen cylinders and medical products were clean for patient use. Our regular staff were finding it hard to fit this important task into their daily schedule.

I decided to reach out to The Flower Cart to see if their organization would have a person who would be suitable for this role. I was familiar with The Flower Cart's ability to meet the work needs of Michelin in Waterville and wondered if their work force would be able to assist us.

In May 2018 Rachel Durno-Allen joined our staff. She arrived with a support worker from The Flower Cart who helped her learn the task and our processes so she would be successful at her new job.

Rachel's responsibility was to make sure our oxygen cylinders and medical equipment were cleaned for our clients who required them. Right away I knew Rachel was going to fit in. She was not scared of hard work and she has demonstrated an excellent work ethic. Rachel requires very little supervision, which all our staff appreciate. She takes direction extremely well and has actually been one of our most independent workers. She knows what to do and then just gets to work doing it."

The partnership between Family 1st Medical and The Flower Cart has been an important part of improving the service Family 1st provides to their community. "By working together," Monette says, "we were able to help The Flower Cart support an individual who just needed an opportunity to shine. As General Manager of Family 1st Medical I would highly recommend The Flower Cart Group to assist any business struggle with labour issues."

THE NEW FACILITY

"The new facility is going to be more than just a bigger version of what we already have," says Randell. "It's a totally different concept in design, going along with the socializing aspect. Each workshop will be like an independent business.

I look at the concepts for this new building and the first reaction is that it's a big, sprawling building, about 23,000 square feet, but it's will also have better ventilation and environmental controls and be way more efficient. It's being built to be more adaptive. What we had served our purposes for a long time, but when you have a building that you can use, designed the way you need it, it's a huge advantage.

We did a community consultation before we started the capital campaign and we heard that many people didn't really know what the Flower Cart did. We collected a lot of feedback and directed a lot more effort into messaging and social media. We've been reaching out to people, and Jeff and I have done a lot of tours with people.

The branding on the building will show our individual enterprises. It's going to look more like a major corporation, but we'll still have the same great work going on inside. We've known that we've needed to expand in order to create more opportunities for a long time. It's exciting to be this close to the finish line."

Though the capital campaign was slowed by the COVID-19 crisis, the timeline has only been delayed, not suspended. "Our original plan was to break ground in the spring of 2021 and we have over two-thirds funds committed. Government at all levels have been a big help, and we received $300,000 from the Municipality of the County of Kings, pledged over 5-years."

"We had a tremendous $100,000 donation from a local business, Nova Industrial, as well as other generous donations from other charities and trusts. All indications are that we'll have almost all of the funds committed by the end of 2020 and be very close to our original timeline.

I certainly think about the future but I'm still looking at the small chunk right now, getting this building going and finished. I think Jean DeWolfe would be very pleased with what she started and where it's gone. It's been fifty years of growth and success, and even if a lot of it happens privately, it's great to get a chance to tell our story.

CHAPTER SEVEN: 2020 VISION

JUDY CROCKER, A PROFILE

Judy Crocker is a 57-year old mother of two from Kentville who commutes to and from The Flower Cart by bus. Prior to becoming a participant, she had taken a course at PeopleWorx in food handling and safety. "My social worker asked if I wanted to do something new and my kids were away in high school, so I decided to give it a try," she says. "I did enjoy my time there."

Judy enjoys reading, doing puzzles, scrapbooking (she's starting one on The Flower Cart) and her regular games of Forty-Fives, but when her time at PeopleWorx came to an end, she was bored. Her social worker advised her to explore the options available at The Flower Cart. She liked what she saw and soon enrolled. "I had taken literacy lessons down the street at the Community Employment building but didn't know much about the organization," she says.

"I spend half my time in the bakery and half in used clothing, but I prefer being downstairs in used clothing. I'm one of the older clients here and it's easier on my legs. I especially like the social contact and I really missed that aspect during the COVID-19 restrictions." Judy has also volunteered at the food bank and worked for Just Us! Coffee and Consigners.

The Flower Cart's Capital Campaign, *Building Opportunities*, has engaged Judy as part of their presentation team when seeking financial support from various public and private organizations. A few minutes in her presence and you can see why she was chosen. She brings the highly credible perspective of the ultimate Flower Cart stakeholder to the table, speaking from personal and practical experience when describing the need for a new facility.

Judy may be soft-spoken but her informed opinions carry a lot of weight. "The current building is getting old and we don't have enough room," she says. "If we had more space we could hire more people. There are a lot of people out there who don't have things to do. I just give my opinion about how to make the new place most effective. It feels good that they asked me to do this. I'm not the only one, three or four others have done that too. We all want a bigger space to allow more people to get out into the community. This building has brought us a long way but it's time for something new."

Judy also makes her quiet-but-respected voice heard in the area of self-advocacy. She points with pride to the eight important goals that the Participant Planning Group have recently identified:

*The right to have help to make my own decisions

*The right to be safe from abuse

*The right to be listened to – no matter how I communicate

*The right to make my own decisions about my life

*The right to relationships

*The right to be treated fairly

*The right to privacy

*The right to information in a way I understand

"We all want to improve how we express ourselves around people," she adds. "I definitely speak up more than I did at first. As long as you know the people in the group, it's not as hard."

As a leader in the Participant Planning Group, Judy encourages her colleagues to say more. "If we think there's something that should be changed, we should be able to tell them - to a certain extent at least. It's okay to disagree if you don't like something. The new facility will make it easier to speak up. It's so important to be able to take things to the right people if something bad is happening to us."

Judy's pet peeve is spending money for repairs of the existing building instead of putting those dollars toward the new facility. She points out that one-third or more of the participants have accessibility problems due to a physical disability. "There are four doors but only one door where they can enter. And the stairs are a real problem, too."

Judy has used the COVID-19 shutdown to improve her computer skills and catch up on her reading. "I'd love to stay at the Flower Cart for a while longer," she says. "The staff is helpful, especially if you're having an off day. The Flower Cart has definitely made my life better. I like learning new things and finding out about different job opportunities. I especially like the companionship and just being around people, that's the biggest thing for me."

A FINAL LOOK BACK

The Flower Cart has now been part of the Valley community for fifty years. It's important and fitting to honour that history and those visionaries, educators, participants, and supporters who have brought us to this point. The founders persevered through hard times and overcame countless obstacles and numerous naysayers to create a place of hope, purpose, and growth.

As important as it is to look back at the 1970 vision, examine the pitfalls, and celebrate the accomplishments, it's equally important to look ahead. The planned new facility is the very public face of that vision and it will be from this bustling centre that the programs and services will evolve over the ensuing decades.

Of course, no look into the future can be completely clear. The COVID-19 pandemic has made that abundantly clear. There will be changes in the way things are done, and the years will undoubtedly bring other unforeseen challenges. As it always has, The Flower

Cart must be ready and able to adapt to those new realities and find a way to keep moving forward.

The need for community support will not diminish. Without the help of dedicated individuals, community organizations, service clubs, and government agencies, The Flower Cart would not have survived five decades. Although great strides have been made in gaining financial self-sufficiency, the greater Annapolis Valley community will continue to play a vital role. The Flower Cart sprang from the community and received its nurture from Valley people and organizations. In the intervening years those roots have deepened and spread across all sectors. Generosity of spirit infuses every aspect of The Flower Cart.

Businesses, big and small, have come to see the advantages of partnerships with The Flower Cart. Led by progressive, informed businesspeople, they have been able to look beyond the antiquated stereotypes and see opportunity where once they saw roadblocks. The Annapolis Valley business community, from start-up companies to small Mom-and-Pop businesses to world class corporations have discovered the wisdom of employing Flower Cart trainees to help them grow.

The new facility will only enhance this growth as the general public discovers the hidden dimensions of the sheltered workshop they think they know. The facility will be multi-faceted, both in the diversity of services offered and in the benefits for participants. The bakery will provide healthy food to the public while continuing to serve as a training vehicle for participants. There will be a café and related outlets that will facilitate the easy mixing of participants and the public, further crushing stereotypes and erasing unhealthy divisions.

"We are primarily a reflection of what our clients need," says Contract Services Coordinator Matt Clairmont. "Because of that, our programs and services evolve to changing times and changing needs."

The new Flower Cart building will have the appearance of a professional business in the service sector. It will command the attention of citizens and businesses alike and send the unmistakable message that The Flower Cart is a major player. It is designed to reflect a very different sensibility than the one that existed when the doors of the old elementary school were opened to a brave new idea. That repurposed building served its clients well, underwent many renovations and expansions to fit changing programmes and expanding enrollments, but it is time for a new home.

Participants and staff need room to grow and innovate. They look forward to more independence at the opportunity to provide greater support. With so many senior staff retiring or entering the final phases of their career with The Flower Cart Group, the focus shifts to mentorship and succession planning, and ensuring that the culture of participant-focus is captured and carried on.

Asked to imagine what the future could and should hold for The Flower Cart, former executive director Roger Tatlock stresses the importance of looking back in order to look forward. "The center of all this is the vision," he says. "That is the one constant, that founding document that Jean DeWolfe and that board wrote in 1974. When you read that you see that everything cascades from it. It provided that initial push."

"The laws of physics say that a body in motion tends to stay in motion, so let's keep the thing going. Jack Wendt, back when he was on the board, said 'Roger, in 2020 they are going to have to write the fifty thing – the 2020 vision. It's the vision of the past but more importantly the vision of the future.'

You have a foundation and you know the foundation. How we've added to that foundation should be an indication of whether the vision has been successful. Ask yourself, what is your contribution to its continued growth? You being the staff, you being the executive director, you being the board member, you being a member of the Rotary Club, you being the dean of the Education Department, you being the professor who's teaching social enterprise, in the school of business education, you being the head of the community college human service counsellor program, and you being a citizen of the Annapolis Valley – how are you moving this vision forward?

This community made these things happen. This is your fight, this is your covenant. How are you going to be moving it forward? How are you going to do more? And aren't you in 2020 as excited as the people who wrote this back in 1974? Look where you came from! People living in the Big House up on the hill in the middle of nowhere and now Michelin can't make a tire in Nova Scotia without The Flower Cart."

When the doors of The Flower Cart first opened to admit 4 young ladies in the fall of 1970, few of the organizers could have foreseen a time, fifty years hence, when the participants, now numbering in the hundreds, would be working in a variety of jobs throughout the county and earning a living doing so.

Even fewer would have predicted that The Flower Cart participants would have a degree of autonomy and self-advocacy in decision making and the mapping out of their own future.

By today's standards, the original goals of The Flower Cart may seem modest, but only when viewed with the advantage of hindsight. The bold core of community activists who conceived and built The Flower Cart were looking ahead, as all good visionaries must, because pioneers don't have the luxury of hindsight.

The first steps were tentative ones, "baby steps" as Tatlock calls them, but they were always moving in the right direction. They were breaking new ground and learning on the job. Tatlock is amazed at how relevant the mission statement remains, five decades later. There are differences in language obviously, and in approaches, certainly, but the fundamental vision is the same.

In 2020, the goals revolve around the concept of social enterprise and finding people with a social conscience to move things from traditional to more purpose-driven businesses.

"The mission hasn't changed that much but how we carry out that mission has," says current executive director Jeff Kelly. "The future is based on paid employment. It represents almost 60% of our profits. That's the premier focus, paid employment within social enterprise. There are a variety of barriers to mainstream employment and we need logistical support to get there, but we always find a way."

The terminology has changed, and the methodologies have evolved. Executive directors, board members, and staff have come and gone, as have thousands of participants. Even the physical structure that has served as the beating heart of The Flower Cart is about to be replaced. What can't be replaced are fifty years of experience, learning, trying and failing, persistence, and dedication. The next fifty years will be a continuation of this journey. Exactly what it will look like is impossible to predict.

The challenge, which has become abundantly clear in the creation of this retrospective, is defining The Flower Cart when it is so many things to so many people. So many talented, industrious, and insightful men and women have come in and left their mark. So many participants, dismayed by a world focused on what they can't do, have found themselves embraced by an organization focused on what they can. So many have made important and crucial breakthroughs, developed strategies for managing change, and continued on a path of lifelong learning.

The hope is that the essence of The Flower Cart remains. Bricks and mortar are a by-product and a conduit of change, but the vision set out by the founders is still valid and it will endure.

Ultimately it is this list of extraordinary people, too exhaustive to include here, that has shaped The Flower Cart, and it is their extraordinary efforts that will see it go bravely into the next fifty years.

www.ingramcontent.com/pod-product-compliance
Lightning Source LLC
Chambersburg PA
CBHW070839250726

48662CB00003B/1292